PRAYERS AND PROMISES
FOR EVERY DAY

Joyce Morris

By the same author

The Hiding Place

Prayers and Promises for Every Day

from The Living Bible

with

Corrie ten Boom

Hodder & Stoughton

LONDON SYDNEY AUCKLAND

All quotations used in the daily scripture selections are from
The Living Bible, copyright © 1971 by Tyndale House Publishers,
Wheaton, Illinois 60187. Used by permission.

Grateful acknowledgement is made to Christian Literature Crusade
for permission to quote excerpts from the following books by
Corrie ten Boom:

Amazing Love © 1953 CLC
A Prisoner And Yet . . . © 1954
Not Good If Detached © 1946 CLC
Marching Orders For The End Battle © 1969 CLC

Copyright © Harold Shaw Publishers 1977

First published in Great Britain 1978
This edition 1998

British Library Cataloguing in Publication Data
A record for this book is available from the British Library

ISBN 0 340 70995 2

Printed and bound in Great Britain by
Clays Ltd, St Ives plc

Hodder and Stoughton Ltd
A Division of Hodder Headline PLC
338 Euston Road
London NW1 3BH

Introduction

*Jesus Christ ... isn't one to say 'yes' when he means 'no'.
He always does exactly what he says. He carries out and
fulfils all of God's promises, no matter how many of them
there are.* (2 Cor. 1:19, 20).

How often we cry out to God in times of crisis, small
or great, and wish we could *hear his voice answering us,*
assuring us of his help and presence!

The Bible is full of such cries for help from men and
women just like us. Praise God that his Word is also
filled with his answers! He gives us sure promises which
fit every situation in our lives. In this book of daily
readings, individual prayers are coupled with appropriate promises from God in such a way that as we read
them, we can apply them to our own circumstances,
claiming them, 'standing on' them, hearing God's voice
to us in them.

Along with these Prayers and Promises from *The
Living Bible* we have included excerpts from Corrie ten
Boom's writings which demonstrate God's super-
natural answers to human needs and show how Miss
ten Boom was able to apply His promises in her own
life and ministry. She explains:

'The Bible is a cheque book. When you said "yes" to Jesus Christ, many promises were deposited to your credit at that very moment, and they were signed by the Lord Jesus Himself. But now you have to cash your cheques in order to profit by them. When you come upon such a promise and say, "Thank you, Lord, I accept this," then you have cashed a cheque, and that very day you'll be richer than you were the day before.' We encourage you to begin today to enrich your life with God's words of promise!

Luci Shaw

January

■ *I spoke [once] on the reality of the promises of God. Often we do not understand these promises. They seem too lofty and beyond our comprehension, and so we lay them aside without really giving them serious thought. But that is not God's intention. He is back of every promise with His love and His omnipotence, and He was in great earnest when He made them. Therefore I believe that we are sinning when we ignore them or perhaps evade them by theologising them away. (Amazing Love.)*

1

Prayer Hold me safe above the heads of all my enemies. (*Ps. 119:117.*)

Promise I will uphold you with my victorious right hand. (*Is. 46:10.*)

2

Prayer Make me walk along the right paths. (*Ps. 119:133.*)

Promise The steps of good men are directed by the Lord. (*Ps. 37:23.*)

3

Prayer If you aren't going with us, don't let us move a step from this place. (*Ex. 33:15.*)

Promise I myself will go with you and give you success. (*Ex. 33:14.*)

4

Prayer Don't just condemn me — tell me why you are doing it! (*Job 10:2.*)

Promise There is now no condemnation awaiting those who belong to Christ Jesus. (*Rom. 8:1.*)

5

Prayer Come, O Lord, and make me well. In your kindness save me. (*Ps. 6:4.*)

Promise Your faith has healed you. Go in peace. (*Luke 8:48.*)

6

Prayer Lord, lead me as you promised me you would ... tell me clearly what to do, which way to turn. (*Ps. 5:8.*)

Promise I will not be afraid, for you are close beside me, guarding, guiding all the way. (*Ps. 23:4.*)

7

Prayer Don't forsake me, O God of my salvation. (*Ps. 27:9.*)

Promise I will never, *never* fail you or forsake you. (*Heb. 13:5.*)

■ *There was to be a dinner party in a beautiful home beside a river. I had spoken the night before on the subject, 'The problem of sin has been solved on the Cross of Jesus Christ.' And I was glad to see that Jack was present to-night, because I had seen a look of obvious distaste on his face during my talk the night before.*

And now Jack said, 'I believe that there is remission of sins through Jesus Christ, but redemption? No, I can't see that. We have to carry the consequences of our sins as long as we live.'

After dinner we continued our talk in the garden. There were only three of us now; John, with whom I had been working for the past two weeks, and Jack, who was relating his experiences to us. It was a sad story.

'We were not very good boys in high school. I dated a lot of different girls, and one time things went wrong. I had to marry the girl; and four months later the baby came. I want to become a minister; but if people hear about this my whole career will be gone. I am living a lie, and don't know what to do about it. I'll have to bear the consequences of my sin as long as I live.' As he spoke I continued praying for wisdom. Then John began to speak.

'Nevertheless there is redemption. Jesus does not patch things up. He renews. If you will ask Him to go back with you to that dark spot in your life, He will change its darkness into light.'

'But what must I do?' asked Jack. 'I have been converted, as people call it, and I have accepted Jesus as my personal Saviour.'

'You still have to surrender your life completely to Him. Turn over all the keys of your life to Him.'

'I am willing to do it, but I don't know how to express it,' said he.

'Just ask the Spirit of God to give you the right words.' All three of us then prayed, and Jack said, 'I don't understand these things, but here I am, Lord, I know that You have said "Him that cometh unto Me I will in no wise cast out", and "A broken and a contrite heart, O God, Thou wilt not despise." '

Just then I was called into the house. An hour later as I was leaving, Jack said to me, 'Corrie, I can laugh again; I haven't been able to laugh for a year. But now I am free.' And I knew that it was true. (Amazing Love.)

8

Prayer But Lord, my sins! How many they are. Oh, pardon them for the honour of your name. (*Ps. 25:11.*)

Promise If we confess our sins to him, he can be depended on to forgive us, and to cleanse us from every wrong. (*1 John 1:9.*)

9

Prayer Help me to prefer obedience to making money! (*Ps. 119:36.*)

Promise I will inscribe my laws upon their hearts, so that they shall *want* to honour me. (*Jer. 31:33.*)

10

Prayer Search me, O God, and know my heart; test my thoughts. (*Ps. 139:23.*)
Promise He searches all hearts and examines deepest motives. (*Jer. 17:10.*)

11

Prayer My problems go from bad to worse. Oh, save me from them all! (*Ps. 25:17.*)
Promise Be really glad — because these trials will make you partners with Christ in his suffering. (*1 Pet. 4:13.*)

12

Prayer Don't let the floods overwhelm me, or the ocean swallow me; save me from the pit that threatens me. (*Ps. 69:15.*)
Promise When you go through deep waters and great trouble, I will be with you. When you go through rivers of difficulty, you will not drown! (*Is. 43:2.*)

13

Prayer I have wandered away like a lost sheep; come and find me. (*Ps. 119:176.*)
Promise The Lord God says: I will search and find my sheep. (*Ezek. 34:11.*)

14

Prayer Rescue me! Bend down your ear and listen to my plea and save me. (*Ps. 71:2.*)
Promise Yes, he will save the humble. (*Job 22:29.*)

■ *At a conference of Bible school students it is necessary to have somebody to interpret for me, and this is done by a girl who finds it difficult to understand my English. When I use an illustration involving radar in ships she becomes quite mixed up, as she has never heard of radar before.*

'It doesn't matter; we will try something else. A captain of a ship stood on the bridge . . .' but she has never heard of the bridge of a ship, and does not say a word. She bursts into tears. A Japanese who loses face is lost; you cannot do anything with him. I ask the leader of the conference if there is another interpreter, but he tells me there is not.

Here is the devil at work. The first step on the way to victory is to recognise the enemy. I turn to the girl and say:

'Dark power that hinders this girl from interpreting God's message — I command you in the name of the Lord Jesus to leave her alone. She is meant to be a temple of the Holy Spirit, not your temple.'

As I speak, the girl is set free. She is able to interpret fluently, and we have a meeting that is greatly blessed. So what the devil has meant to be an illustration of his victory becomes a boomerang and shows the power of Jesus Christ and His name. (Not Good If Detached.)

15

Prayer   Keep me from all evil and disaster! (*1 Chron. 4:10.*)

Promise   But the Lord is faithful; he will make you strong and guard you from satanic attacks of every kind. (*2 Thess. 3:3.*)

16

Prayer   Come from the four winds, O Spirit, and breathe upon these slain bodies, that they may live again. (*Ezek. 37:9.*)

Promise   The time is coming, in fact, it is here, when the dead shall hear my voice — the voice of the Son of God — and those who listen shall live. (*John 5:25.*)

17

Prayer   Oh, that you would wonderfully bless me! (*1 Chron. 4:10.*)

Promise   The Lord will give you an abundance of good things . . . he will bless everything you do. (*Deut. 28:11, 12.*)

18

Prayer   O Lord, don't stay away. O God, my strength, hurry to my aid. (*Ps. 22:19.*)

Promise   I still love him. I long for him and surely will have mercy on him. (*Jer. 31:20.*)

19

Prayer   Remember me too, O Lord, while you are blessing and saving your people. (*Ps. 106:4.*)

Promise   I will satisfy him with a full life and give him my salvation. (*Ps. 91:16.*)

Prayer   O Lord, don't hold back your tender mercies from me! My only hope is in your love and faithfulness. (*Ps. 40:11.*)

Promise   He protects all those who love him. (*Ps. 145:20.*)

21

Prayer   My God, how I search for you! How I thirst for you in this parched land where there is no water. (*Ps. 63:1.*)

Promise   I will give you abundant water for your thirst and for your parched fields. (*Is. 44:3.*)

■ *A solitary cell awaited me. I was pushed inside and the door closed after me. I was alone. Everything was empty and grey. In the other cell there had been at least the colours of my cell mates' dresses. Here there was nothing, only an emptiness, a cold grey void. I was chilled to the bone. The wind shrieked, and I felt an icy draught through the cell.*

'O Saviour, you are with me. Help me; hold me fast and comfort me. O Saviour, take away this anxiety, this desolation.'

I felt very ill. My fingers and arm throbbed with pain. I could not find a comfortable position.

'Safe in the arms of Jesus. O my Saviour, take me into your arms and comfort me,' I prayed. And peace stole into my heart. The weird noises still surrounded me, but I fell quietly asleep. (A Prisoner And Yet.)

22

Prayer Don't keep looking at my sins — erase them from your sight. (*Ps. 51:9.*)

Promise I've blotted out your sins; they are gone like morning mist at noon! (*Is. 44:22.*)

23

Prayer Tell me where you want me to go and I will go there. (*Ps. 86:11.*)

Promise He will teach the ways that are right and best to those who humbly turn to him. (*Ps. 25:9.*)

24

Prayer We keep on praying for you that our God will make you the kind of children he wants to have — will make you as you wish you could be! (*2 Thess. 1: 11.*)

Promise God who began the good work within you will keep right on helping you grow in his grace until his task within you is finally finished. (*Phil. 1:6.*)

25

Prayer We need more faith; tell us how to get it. (*Luke 17:5.*)

Promise Ask *anything*, using my name, and I will do it! (*John 14:14.*)

Prayer Lord, help us against our enemies, for man's help is useless. (*Ps. 60:11.*)

Promise God has promised to help us. He has vowed it by his holiness. (*Ps. 60:6, 7.*)

27

Prayer Do not disgrace yourself and the throne of your glory by forsaking your promise to bless us! (*Jer. 14:21.*)

Promise No, I will not break my covenant; I will not take back one word of what I said. (*Ps. 89:34.*)

28

Prayer Now bring us back to loving you, O Lord, so that your anger will never need rise against us again. (*Ps. 85:4.*)

Promise I will take from you your hearts of stone and give you tender hearts of love for God, so that you can obey my laws and be my people. (*Ezek. 11:19, 20.*)

29

Prayer Oh, please remember that I'm made of dust. (*Job 10:9.*)

Promise He is like a father to us, tender and sympathetic . . . for he knows we are but dust. (*Ps. 103:13, 14.*)

■ *I was making my way carefully through the mass of people when a young woman bumped into me. She was an acquaintance, and I asked, 'How are you?'*

'I cannot stand it any longer. If I have to stay in this hell for one more week I shall go to pieces.'

'You must not despair, Annie. Jesus is Victor, even if you cannot see it. If you are His, you will be given strength to go on. He will make you see things from God's point of view, and then you will be strong.'

'But what can I do?'

'Surrender yourself to Him. Don't you see that He is standing with arms outstretched; don't you hear Him say, "Come unto Me"?'

Then we prayed. We held each other's hands and had our eyes open. No one who saw us standing there could see that we were praying. All around us was the milling crowd of hundreds of people. When Annie moved on there was an expression of peace on her face. The Lord had heard our prayer. (A Prisoner And Yet.)

30

Prayer Send us around the world with the news of your saving power and your eternal plan for all mankind. (*Ps. 67:2.*)

Promise Go and make disciples in all the nations . . . and be sure of this, that I am with you always. (*Matt. 28:19, 20.*)

31

Prayer Correct me, Lord; but please be gentle. Don't do it in your anger, for I would die. (*Jer. 10:24.*)

Promise Fear not, O Jacob, my servant, says the Lord, for I am with you. I will punish you, but only enough to correct you. (*Jer. 46:28.*)

February

1

Prayer O Lord, have mercy on me in my anguish. My health is broken from sorrow. My sins have sapped my strength. (*Ps. 31:9, 10.*)

Promise I am with you; that is all you need. My power shows up best in weak people. (*2 Cor. 12:9.*)

2

Prayer If God will help and protect me on this journey ... then I will choose Jehovah as my God! (*Gen. 28:20.*)

Promise He orders his angels to protect you wherever you go. (*Ps. 91:11.*)

3

Prayer Lord, save me! (*Ps. 116:4.*)

Promise He rescues you from every trap, and protects you from the fatal plague. (*Ps. 91:3.*)

4

Prayer Because you are so loving and kind, listen to me and make me well again. (*Ps. 119:149.*)

Promise I want to! Be healed! (*Mark 1:41.*)

■ *The name of Jesus is wonderful! Once I heard a story of a sick lady in Germany. A friend asked her:* 'Do you know it is written in the Bible that Jesus said "They will lay their hands upon the sick and they will recover"?' *Then he simply did it. In the name of Jesus he laid his hands on her and she was healed. She was so happy that she went to her pastor and said:* 'Did you know that that text in Mark 16: 18 is in the Bible?' *The pastor's answer was:* 'I am sorry, but I must tell you that that part of Mark 16 was added to the Bible long, long afterwards.' *For one moment she was very disappointed, but suddenly her eyes started to beam with joy and she said:* 'What a wonderful Book is the Bible, that even an added promise has so much power that I was healed!' *(Marching Orders.)*

5

Prayer Seal me in your heart with permanent betrothal. *(Song of Sol. 8:6.)*

Promise I will betroth you to me in faithfulness and love. I will bind you to me forever. *(Hosea 2:20, 19.)*

6

Prayer Pour out your unfailing love on those who know you! *(Ps. 46:10.)*

Promise The Father himself loves you dearly because you love me. *(John 16:27.)*

7

Prayer Teacher, don't you even care that we are all about to drown? *(Mark 4:38.)*

Promise He is always thinking about you and watching everything that concerns you. *(1 Pet. 5:7.)*

8

Prayer Lord, if you keep in mind our sins then who can ever get an answer to his prayers ? (*Ps. 130:3.*)
Promise When you pray, I will listen. You will find me when you seek me. (*Jer. 29:12, 13.*)

9

Prayer O Lord, please help us. Save us. Give us success. (*Ps. 118:25.*)
Promise My Lord ... will send his angel with you and make your mission successful. (*Gen. 24:40.*)

10

Prayer O Lord, do good to those who are good, whose hearts are right with the Lord. (*Ps. 125:4.*)
Promise He caused the good to walk a steady trail like mountain goats upon the rocks. (*2 Sam. 22:34.*)

11

Prayer Lord, I lift my hands to heaven and implore your help. Oh, listen to my cry. (*Ps. 28:2.*)
Promise Go directly to the Father and ask him and he will give you what you ask for because you use my name. (*John 16:23.*)

■ *At four o'clock in the morning we arrived at Vught.*
The women were made to undress, were sent into the showers twenty at a time. Soldiers were walking around staring at the undressed women who had to wait for their showers.

Betsie and I threw our arms around each other and pleaded, 'O Lord, not that.'

'Stop bathing,' came the command. There were not enough gowns.

We shed tears of gratitude. Our turn had not yet come; and when, ten days later, we were given our prison gowns we were alone with the friendly girls of the dressing room, and there was nothing unpleasant or mean about it. God answers prayers. (A Prisoner And Yet.)

12

Prayer But I am in deep trouble. Rush to my aid, for only you can help and save me. O Lord, don't delay. (*Ps. 70:5.*)

Promise For I am offering you my deliverance; not in the distant future, but right now! I am ready to save you. (*Is. 46:13.*)

13

Prayer Oh, do not hold us guilty for our former sins! (*Ps. 79:8.*)

Promise He has removed our sins as far away from us as the east is from the west. (*Ps. 103:12.*)

14

Prayer Heal me, for my body is sick. (*Ps. 6:2.*)

Promise I will give you back your health again and heal your wounds. (*Jer. 30:17.*)

15

Prayer Satisfy us in our earliest youth with your loving kindness, giving us constant joy to the end of our lives. (*Ps. 90:14.*)

Promise I will satisfy my people with my bounty, says the Lord. (*Jer. 31:14.*)

16

Prayer Encourage and cheer me with your words. (*Ps. 119:28.*)

Promise Your words are a flashlight to light the path ahead of me and keep me from stumbling. (*Ps. 119: 105.*)

17

Prayer Lord, how great is your mercy; oh, give me back my life again. (*Ps. 119:156.*)

Promise He fills my life with good things! My youth is renewed like the eagle's! (*Ps. 103:5.*)

18

Prayer You have given us your laws to obey — oh, how I want to follow them consistently. (*Ps. 119:5.*)

Promise For God is at work within you, helping you want to obey him and then helping you do what he wants. (*Phil. 2:13.*)

■ *It is a wonderful life that is guided by a God who never makes mistakes. The only condition laid upon us is obedience.*

In my Quiet Time the instruction comes distinctly, 'Go to Japan.' I almost answer, 'Yes, but . . .' Obedience says, 'Yes, Lord,' and I have learned to obey. I want to say, 'Yes, but I know nobody there; I can't speak the language and it is so expensive.' Again and again I begin counting and forget that my heavenly Treasurer reckons differently from me. The money comes, enough for a flight to Tokyo, where I arrive safely.

It is raining, and from the air Tokyo looks dark and dreary. I am not at all sure of myself. In the customs office a man asks me where he is to take my suitcase. I tell him I do not know.

Now there is a conflict in my soul. Was that really God's guidance? What if it was a mistake?

How it happens I cannot explain, but trust takes the place of doubt, and I can say, 'Lord, I know I am safe in Your everlasting arms. You are guiding me and will surely make the next step plain.'

Then comes to mind: 'David Morken.' Is that God's answer? Years ago I met David at a Youth for Christ meeting, and he told me then that he might be sent to Japan. Fortunately the telephone directory is printed in English, and there is his name, 'David Morken, Director of Youth for Christ, Tokyo.'

How wonderful, for now the next step is clear. I pick up the telephone and speak to David Morken. That day I am his guest, after which he secures a room for me in an Inter-Varsity Christian Fellowship house.

The first week I speak three times, the second week eighteen times, and the third week twenty-six times. A season of unusual blessing awaits me. How happy I am that I said, 'Yes, Lord,' instead of 'Yes, but . . .' (Not Good If Detached.)

19

Prayer Help me to do your will. (*Ps. 143:10.*)
Promise If anyone keeps looking steadily into God's law . . . he will not only remember it but will do what it says. (*James 1:25.*)

20

Prayer Oh, help us, Lord our God! For we trust in you alone. (*2 Chron. 14:11.*)
Promise Because they trust in him, he helps them and delivers them. (*Ps. 37:40.*)

21

Prayer Give me an understanding mind. (*1 Kings 3: 9.*)
Promise He will change disobedient minds to the wisdom of faith. (*Luke 1:17.*)

22

Prayer Give us our food again, today, as usual. (*Matt. 6:11.*)
Promise Food will be supplied to them and they will have all the water they need. (*Is. 33:16.*)

23

Prayer Reassure me that your promises are for me, for I trust and revere you. (*Ps. 119:38.*)
Promise I will reaffirm my covenant with you, and you will know I am the Lord. (*Ezek. 16:62.*)

24

Prayer   Let the Lord our God favour us and give us success. (*Ps. 90:17.*)

Promise   If you are careful to obey every one of [God's laws] you will be successful in everything you do. (*Josh. 1:7.*)

25

Prayer   Lord, save us! We're sinking! (*Matt. 8:25.*)

Promise   Not a hair of your head will perish! (*Luke 21:18.*)

■ *A Hollander, Mrs. DeBoer, approached me one evening. 'Corrie, can you help me? I am afraid. I've just seen a woman cruelly beaten to death. I am afraid of death. Do help me. Perhaps you can tell me something from your Book that will take away this terrible fear.'*

'Yes, indeed I can,' I replied. 'This Book has the answer in John 1:12, "As many as received Him, to them gave He power to become the sons of God".'

'That says nothing to me,' answered Mrs. DeBoer. 'When you say I must accept Jesus I simply don't know what you mean.'

I prayed for wisdom.

'Do you recall years ago when Mr. DeBoer proposed to you? How did you answer him?'

She smiled sadly and replied, 'I said, "Yes".'

'Exactly. And when you had spoken that one little word you belonged to one another, you to him and he to you.'

We sat quietly for a few moments, and then together we prayed. She, too, prayed and gave her answer to Jesus — 'Yes.' (Not Good If Detached.)

26

Prayer Take your shield and protect me by standing in front. Lift your spear in my defence. (*Ps. 35:2, 3.*)
Promise What blessings are yours, O Israel! Who else has been saved by the Lord? He is your shield and your helper! He is your excellent sword! (*Deut. 33:29.*)

27

Prayer Overlook my youthful sins, O Lord! Look at me instead through eyes of mercy and forgiveness, through eyes of everlasting love and kindness. (*Ps. 25: 7.*)
Promise I will be merciful to them in their wrong-doings, and I will remember their sins no more. (*Heb. 8:12.*)

28

Prayer All night long I search for you; earnestly I seek for God. (*Is. 26:9.*)
Promise Yes, says the Lord, I will be found by you ... when you seek me, if you will look for me in earnest. (*Jer. 29:14, 13.*)

29

Prayer Save me, O my God. The floods have risen. Deeper and deeper I sink in the mire. (*Ps. 69:1.*)
Promise All who listen to my instructions and follow them are wise, like a man who builds his house on solid rock. (*Matt. 7:26.*)

March

1

Prayer   Come, Lord, and show me your mercy, for I am helpless, overwhelmed, in deep distress. (*Ps. 25:16.*)
Promise   See, I am for you, and I will come and help you. (*Ezek. 36:9.*)

2

Prayer   Create in me a new, clean heart, O God, filled with clean thoughts and right desires. (*Ps. 51:10.*)
Promise   I will give you a new heart — I will give you new and right desires — and put a new spirit within you. (*Ezek. 36:26.*)

3

Prayer   Rescue me from those who hunt me down relentlessly. (*Ps. 31:15.*)
Promise   I will rescue you and free you from the grip of your enemies. (*Mic. 4:10.*)

■ *Then came the ordeal of passing through the gate. On either side were officers and a number of Aufseherinnen.*

The men looked like wild animals feeding on their prey.
When one woman failed to keep her arms stretched out
before her, one of the officers pounced on her, dragged her
out of the line, and beat her cruelly. It seemed to be nothing
more than a fiendish demonstration of his cowardly daring
before the others, who looked with pleasure and approval
upon his treatment of a weak woman. Another 'stalwart'
officer pulled a small bag out of the hands of an old woman
and threw it on the ground with a curse. What an experi-
ence it was to pass through the gate with an 'honour guard'
of such depraved people on either side of us!

'I shall preserve thy going out and thy coming in,' said
the Lord to me. I looked up; small, fleecy-white clouds,
tinged with red, moved like a flock of sheep across the sky.
Then we were on the road. (A Prisoner And Yet.)

4

Prayer Come and save me from these men of the
world. (*Ps. 17:13.*)
Promise Because they trust in him, he helps them
and delivers them from the plots of evil men. (*Ps. 37:
40.*)

5

Prayer Be gracious to us and receive us. (*Hos. 14:2.*)
Promise Leave them; separate yourselves from
them; don't touch their filthy things, and I will
welcome you. (*2 Cor. 6:17.*)

6

Prayer Restore to me again the joy of your salvation. (*Ps. 51:12.*)

Promise Weeping may go on all night, but in the morning there is joy. (*Ps. 30:5.*)

7

Prayer Oh, be not so angry with us, Lord, nor forever remember our sins. (*Is. 64:9.*)

Promise I will not fight against you forever, nor always show my wrath. (*Is. 57:16.*)

8

Prayer Keep me from deliberate wrongs; help me to stop doing them. (*Ps. 19:13.*)

Promise Sin need never again be your master. (*Rom. 6:14*).

9

Prayer Praise God, O world! May all the peoples of the earth give thanks to you. (*Ps. 67:5.*)

Promise I have made Israel for myself, and these my people will some day honour me before the world. (*Is. 43:21.*)

10

Prayer Lord, if you keep in mind our sins then who can ever get an answer to his prayers? (*Ps. 130:3.*)

Promise He has removed our sins as far away from us as the east is from the west. He is like a father to us, tender and sympathetic to those who reverence him. (*Ps. 103:12, 13.*)

■ *To a group of political prisoners I speak about the forgiveness of sins. The next day a letter written in perfect Dutch comes with the request, 'Will you write to your Queen for me? She is the only one who can grant me amnesty.' The writer is one of 260 Japanese prisoners sentenced by the Dutch Government for war crimes in Indonesia, once the Dutch East Indies. They are now in a Japanese prison.*

'What must I do, Lord?' I ask.

The answer comes clearly. 'Ask amnesty not only for this man, but for all 260.' I go to the Consul to seek his help in composing my letter, for it is not every day I write to a queen. 'These men are guilty,' I write, 'but in you they see the Christian monarch of a Christian country. Perhaps they can better understand the mercy of our Lord Jesus if you can see your way clear to grant them their freedom, and so it will be to God's glory and honour.'

The Queen sends me the answer that she will do her utmost to see that my request is granted. The men are freed. (Not Good If Detached.)

11

Prayer   O Lord, please help us. Save us. Give us success. (*Ps. 118:25.*)
Promise   Great is the Lord who enjoys helping his child! (*Ps. 35:27.*)

12

Prayer   O Lord, do good to those who are good, whose hearts are right with the Lord. (*Ps. 125:4.*)
Promise   I will rejoice to do them good. (*Jer. 32:41.*)

13

Prayer My health is broken beneath my sins. They are like a flood, higher than my head; they are a burden too heavy to bear. (*Ps. 38:4.*)

Promise Give your burdens to the Lord. He will carry them. (*Ps. 55:22.*)

14

Prayer Oh, please pardon my sin now. (*1 Sam. 15: 25.*)

Promise I will never again remember their sins. (*Heb. 10:17.*)

15

Prayer You have saved me from death and my feet from slipping. (*Ps. 56:13.*)

Promise He will protect his godly ones. (*1 Sam. 2: 9.*)

16

Prayer Rise up, O Lord, and come and help us. Save us by your constant love. (*Ps. 44:26.*)

Promise Don't be afraid, for I have ransomed you; I have called you by name; you are mine. (*Is. 43:1.*)

17

Prayer Defend your people, Lord; defend and bless your chosen ones. (*Ps. 28:19.*)

Promise You can be sure that I will rescue my people. (*Zech. 8:7.*)

■ *I often wonder how it is possible that so many Christians live like beggars when we are Royal children, the very children of God. We appropriate one or two of His promises, but most of them we negate, or ignore, or — reject.*

If indeed we have been 'blessed with all spiritual blessings in heavenly places in Christ' (Eph. 1:3), why then do we still so often sigh? Are we really saved? Or is the devil right when he accuses us day and night? Is it true that we have been made 'the righteousness of God in Christ'? (II Cor. 5:21).

Nietzsche has said, 'Maybe I would have believed in a Redeemer if the Christians had looked more redeemed.' Is it not written in Romans 5:5, 'The love of God is shed abroad in our hearts by the Holy Ghost which is given unto us.' Why, then, do people not see that love in our eyes? We so often live like carnal Christians. (Amazing Love.)

18

Prayer O my God, you are my helper. You are my Saviour; come quickly, and save me. (*Ps. 40:17.*)

Promise I am coming soon to rescue you. (*Is. 56:1.*)

19

Prayer Give us that bread every day of our lives! (*John 6:34.*)

Promise I am that Living Bread that came down out of heaven. Anyone eating this Bread shall live forever. (*John 6:51.*)

20

Prayer Reach down from heaven and rescue me; deliver me from deep waters, from the power of my enemies. (*Ps. 144:7.*)

Promise He will deliver you again and again, so that no evil can touch you. (*Job 5:19.*)

21

Prayer Rescue me and give me back my life again just as you have promised. (*Ps. 119:154.*)

Promise Yes, God often does these things for man — brings back his soul from the pit, so that he may live in the light of the living. (*Job 33:29, 30.*)

22

Prayer Give me happiness, O Lord, for I worship only you. (*Ps. 86:4.*)

Promise You have sorrow now, but I will see you again and then you will rejoice; and no one can rob you of that joy. (*John 16:22.*)

23

Prayer O Lord, don't hold back your tender mercies from me! My only hope is in your love and faithfulness. (*Ps. 40:11.*)

Promise Jehovah God is our Light and our Protector. He gives us grace and glory. No good thing will he withhold from those who walk along his path. (*Ps. 84: 11.*)

Prayer Oh, what a terrible predicament I'm in! Who will free me from my slavery to this deadly lower nature ? (*Rom. 7:24*.)

Promise God took the sinless Christ and poured into him our sins. Then, in exchange, he poured God's goodness into us. (*2 Cor. 5:21*.)

■ *In London I was asked to call on a woman in a mental institution. Her husband had been kind to the Jews, and then it was the Jews who had dropped a bomb on their home. When she regained consciousness and saw that her husband was dead, she opened her heart to hatred. Now she was a complete wreck. She spent the whole day reading the newspapers in order to find news about the Jews. If something terrible happened to them she was happy.*

As she entered the room she looked suspiciously at me. I prayed for wisdom and love.

'I know exactly what you're going to tell me. I must banish the hatred from my heart, because only then can I pray again.'

'Who has told you that?'

'The chaplain.'

'No doubt the chaplain is still a very young man, and he does not yet know how powerful the devil of hatred is. You and I know. Once I was with my sister in a concentration camp. When they treated me cruelly I could stand it, but when I saw that they intended to beat my sister, because she was too weak to shovel sand, then hatred tried to enter my heart. And then I experienced a miracle. Jesus

had planted His love in my heart, and there was no room left for hatred. If it is dark in a room, while the sun is shining outside, do I have to sweep the darkness out? Of course not. I merely have to draw the curtains aside, and as soon as the sunlight floods the room the darkness vanishes.'

We both knelt down, and I prayed, 'Lord, here we are, weak, much weaker than the devil of hatred. But Thou art stronger than the devil of hatred, and now we open our hearts to Thee, and we give thanks to Thee that Thou art willing to enter into our hearts, as the sun is willing to flood a room that is opened to its brightness.'

A week later the woman was discharged from the mental institution. Her heart was full of the love of God. (Amazing Love.)

25

Prayer   May we be refreshed as by streams in the desert. (*Ps. 126:4.*)
Promise   The water I give them ... becomes a perpetual spring within them, watering them forever with eternal life. (*John 4:14.*)

26

Prayer   Help me to love your every wish. (*Ps. 119: 80.*)
Promise   God is at work within you, helping you want to obey him. (*Phil. 2:13.*)

27

Prayer   Show me where to walk. (*Ps. 143:8.*)

Promise   The Lord watches over all the plans and paths of godly men. (*Ps. 1:6.*)

28

Prayer   I reach out for you. I thirst for you as parched land thirsts for rain. (*Ps. 143:6.*)

Promise   For I will give you abundant water for your thirst and for your parched fields. And I will pour out my Spirit and my blessings on your children. (*Is. 44:3.*)

29

Prayer   Protect me as you would the pupil of your eye; hide me in the shadow of your wings as you hover over me. My enemies encircle me with murder in their eyes. (*Ps. 17:8, 9.*)

Promise   Just as the mountains surround and protect Jerusalem, so the Lord surrounds and protects his people. (*Ps. 125:2.*)

30

Prayer   O Lord, . . . no one else can help us! Here we are, powerless against this mighty army. Oh, help us, Lord our God! Don't let mere men defeat you! (*2 Chron. 14:11.*)

Promise   He gives power to the tired and worn out, and strength to the weak. (*Is. 40:29.*)

Prayer Listen to my pleading, Lord! Be merciful and send the help I need. (*Ps. 27:7.*)

Promise I will answer them before they even call to me. While they are still talking to me about their needs, I will go ahead and answer their prayers. (*Is. 65:24.*)

■ *When I was in a prison camp in Holland during the last World War I often prayed: 'Lord, never let the enemy put me in a German concentration camp.' God answered 'No' to that prayer, but in the German camp we were among many prisoners who had never heard of Jesus Christ. If God had not used Betsie and me to bring them to Him, they would never have heard of Him. Many of them died, or were killed, but many died with the name of Jesus on their lips. They were well worth all our suffering, even Betsie's death. To be used to save souls for eternity is worth living and dying. In that way we saw God's side, and could thank Him for unanswered prayer. (Not Good If Detached.)*

April

1

Prayer Guide me clearly along the way you want me to travel so that I will understand you and walk acceptably. (*Ex. 33:13.*)

Promise I myself will go with you and give you success. (*Ex. 33:14.*)

2

Prayer How long will you forget me, Lord? Forever? (*Ps. 13:2.*)

Promise I will not forget you. (*Is. 49:15.*)

3

Prayer I will praise the Lord no matter what happens. (*Ps. 34:1.*)

Promise We know that all that happens to us is working for our good if we love God and are fitting into his plans. (*Rom. 8:28.*)

4

Prayer O God enthroned above the cherubim, bend down your ear and listen as I plead. Display your power and radiant glory. (*Ps. 80:1.*)

Promise For you who fear my name, the Sun of Righteousness will rise with healing in his wings. (*Mal. 4:2.*)

5

Prayer The longing of my heart and my prayer is that the Jewish people might be saved. (*Rom. 10:1.*)

Promise When I am lifted up [on the cross] I will draw everyone to me. (*John 12:32.*)

6

Prayer Holy Father, keep them in your own care — all those you have given me — so that they will be united just as we are. (*John 17:11.*)

Promise Whoever lives in me and I in him shall produce a large crop of fruit. For apart from me you can't do a thing. (*John 15:5.*)

7

Prayer Tell me what to do, O Lord, and make it plain. (*Ps. 27:11.*)

Promise I will instruct you (says the Lord) and guide you along the best pathway for your life; I will advise you and watch your progress. (*Ps. 32:8.*)

■ *Returning to Holland after my release from the German concentration camp at Ravensbruck, I said, 'One*

*thing I hope is that I'll never have to go to Germany
again. I am willing to go wherever God may want me to
go; but I hope He'll never send me to Germany.'*

*On my trips to the United States I often spoke on the
conditions in Europe during the post-war years, and when
I talked of the chaos in Germany, people sometimes asked
me 'Why don't you go to Germany, since you know the
language?' But I didn't want to go.*

*Then darkness came into my fellowship with God;
when I asked for His guidance, there was no answer. Now
God does not want us ever to be in doubt as to what His
guidance is, and so I knew that something had come between God and me, and I prayed, 'Lord is there some
disobedience in my life?' The answer was very distinct:
'Germany.'*

*'Yes, Lord, I'll go to Germany, too. I'll follow where-
ever you lead.' (Amazing Love.)*

8

Prayer Now give me wisdom and knowledge. (*2
Chron. 1:10.*)
Promise He is always ready to give a bountiful
supply of wisdom to all who ask him. (*James 1:5.*)

9

Prayer Deliver us from the Evil One. (*Matt. 6:13.*)
Promise You will tread our sins beneath your feet.
(*Mic. 7:19.*)

10

Prayer   Let me hear you say that you will save me. (*Ps. 35:3.*)

Promise   You will know at last and really understand that I, the Lord, am your Saviour and Redeemer, the Mighty One of Israel. (*Is. 60:16.*)

11

Prayer   Yes, be exalted, O God, above the heavens. May your glory shine throughout the earth. (*Ps. 57:11.*)

Promise   Stand silent! Know that I am God! I will be honoured by every nation in the world! (*Ps. 46:10.*)

12

Prayer   Grant strength to your servant. (*Ps. 86:16.*)

Promise   He will give his people strength. (*Ps. 29: 11.*)

13

Prayer   Remember me too, O Lord, while you are blessing and saving your people. (*Ps. 106:4.*)

Promise   For you bless the godly man, O Lord; you protect him with your shield of love. (*Ps. 5:11.*)

14

Prayer   Make everyone rejoice who puts his trust in you. (*Ps. 5:11.*)

Promise   All the world will see the good hand of God upon his people. (*Is. 66:14.*)

■ *He (God) has told me to go to America, but I find that many papers are needed. I must visit so many offices. This* is the first difficult test of obedience to the guidance upon which I now depend. When my parents were married they were given the verse, 'I will guide thee with Mine eye' (*Ps. 32:8*). This promise becomes my special directive for all my journeyings.

Wherever I go, the answer is, 'No papers are available for America.'

I pray, 'Lord, if it is Your will that I go to America, they must provide papers.' Again and again God performs a miracle. After some time I have most of the papers in my hand. (*Not Good If Detached.*)

15

Prayer   Lead me; teach me. (*Ps. 25:5.*)

Promise   When the Holy Spirit, who is truth, comes, he shall guide you into all truth. (*John 16:13.*)

16

Prayer   Hear my prayer, O Lord; listen to my cry! Don't sit back, unmindful of my tears. (*Ps. 39:12.*)

Promise   O my people in Jerusalem, you shall weep no more, for he will surely be gracious to you at the sound of your cry. He will answer you. (*Is. 30:19.*)

17

Prayer   Waken! Rouse yourself! Don't sleep, O Lord! Are we cast off forever? (*Ps. 44:23.*)

Promise   The Lord will not forsake his people, for they are his prize. (*Ps. 94:14.*)

18

Prayer You're just trying to scare us into stopping our work. (O Lord God, please strengthen me!) (*Neh. 6:9.*)

Promise Don't be impatient. Wait for the Lord, and he will come and save you! Be brave, stouthearted and courageous. Yes, wait and he will help you. (*Ps. 27:14.*)

19

Prayer Oh, that God would grant the thing I long for most. (*Job 6:8.*)

Promise Be delighted with the Lord. Then he will give you all your heart's desires. (*Ps. 37:4.*)

20

Prayer Please be with me in all that I do. (*1 Chron. 4:10.*)

Promise Be sure of this — that I am with you always, even to the end of the world (*Matt. 28:20.*)

21

Prayer I am close to death at the hands of my enemies; oh, give me back my life again, just as you promised me. (*Ps. 119:107.*)

Promise Don't be afraid, for I have ransomed you ... When you go through rivers of difficulty, you will not drown! When you walk through the fire of oppression, you will not be burned up. (*Is. 43:1, 2.*)

■ *Marching back to the camp, I stumbled rather than walked. And then we still had to pass through the gate.*

'Lord, help Thou me; preserve my going out and my coming in; I plead upon Thy promises,' I prayed. We got safely through. In the barracks I fell exhausted upon my bed. After a half hour of deep sleep I had recovered sufficiently to lead the church service. I spoke on the text: 'Be strong in the Lord, and in the power of His might.' What a joy it was to comfort others and myself with the thought that Jesus was the Victor, and that His strength was fulfilled in weakness. As I spoke about the great love and mercy of the Saviour, I felt myself lifted up and far beyond the camp.

'They that wait upon the Lord shall renew their strength.' (A Prisoner And Yet.)

22

Prayer Bless me with life so that I can continue to obey you. (*Ps. 119:17.*)

Promise You will live in joy and peace. (*Is. 55:12.*)

23

Prayer Turn me again to you and restore me, for you alone are the Lord, my God. (*Jer. 31:18.*)

Promise There shall come out of Zion a Deliverer, and he shall turn the Jews from all ungodliness. (*Rom. 11:26.*)

24

Prayer O Lord my God ... I am as a little child who doesn't know his way around. (*1 Kings 3:7.*)

Promise But I am with you; that is all you need. My power shows up best in weak people. (*2 Cor. 12:9.*)

25

Prayer Save me from being overpowered by my sins. (*Ps. 39:8.*)

Promise All his past sins will be forgotten, and he shall live because of his goodness. (*Ezek. 18:22.*)

26

Prayer Don't turn away from me in this time of my distress. Bend down your ear and give me speedy answers. (*Ps. 102:2.*)

Promise When he calls on me I will answer; I will be with him in trouble, and rescue him and honour him. (*Ps. 91:15.*)

27

Prayer Sprinkle me with the cleansing blood and I shall be clean again. (*Ps. 51:7.*)

Promise If we are living in the light of God's presence, just as Christ does, then ... the blood of Jesus his Son cleanses us from every sin. (*1 John 1:7.*)

28

Prayer O Lord God, please let me cross over into the Promised Land. (*Deut. 3:25.*)

Promise Your eyes will see the King in his beauty, and the highlands of heaven. (*Is. 33:17.*)

■ *I will tell you something that happened when I was a prisoner in a concentration camp with my sister, Betsie. One morning I had a terrible cold, and I said to Betsie, 'What can I do; I have no handkerchief.'*

'Pray,' she said. I smiled, but she prayed, 'Father, Corrie has got a cold, and she has no handkerchief. Will You give her one in Jesus' name, Amen.'

I could not help laughing, but as she said 'Amen,' I heard my name called. I went to the window, and there stood my friend who worked in the prison hospital.

'Quickly, quickly! Take this little package; it is a little present for you.' I opened the package, and inside was a handkerchief. (Not Good If Detached.)

29

Prayer Surround me with your tender mercies, that I may live. (*Ps. 119:77.*)

Promise Through Christ, all the kindness of God has been poured out upon us. (*Rom. 1:5.*)

30

Prayer Let us praise the Lord together, and exalt his name. (*Ps. 34:3.*)

Promise I will honour my great name ... and the people of the world shall know I am the Lord. (*Ezek. 36:23.*)

May

1

Prayer We ask that your kingdom will come now. (*Matt. 6:10.*)

Promise Let him reign from sea to sea, and from the Euphrates River to the ends of the earth. (*Ps. 72:8.*)

2

Prayer We know not what evil we have done; only tell us, and we will cease at once. (*Job 34:32.*)

Promise When the Father sends the Comforter instead of me — and by the Comforter I mean the Holy Spirit — he will teach you much. (*John 14:26.*)

3

Prayer You deserve ... utter sincerity and truthfulness. Oh, give me this wisdom. (*Ps. 51:6.*)

Promise The righteous shall move onward and forward; those with pure hearts shall become stronger and stronger. (*Job 17:9.*)

4

Prayer O send out your light and your truth. (*Ps. 43:3.*)

Promise The wisdom that comes from heaven is first of all pure . . . then it is peaceloving and courteous. (*James 3:17.*)

5

Prayer If only I could die as happy as an Israelite! Oh, that my end might be like theirs! (*Num. 23:10.*)

Promise You shall live a long, good life; like standing grain, you'll not be harvested until it's time! (*Job 5:26.*)

6

Prayer O Lord, arise! Don't forget the poor or anyone else in need. (*Ps. 10:12.*)

Promise He does not ignore the prayers of men in trouble when they call to him for help. (*Ps. 9:12.*)

■ *The nights seem unendurably hot. The unscreened window invites swarms of mosquitoes. Self-pity rises in my heart and whispers, 'Why must I work here when the heat is so overpowering? I'm no longer young, and adjustment does not come easily. Why must I be alone? Why? Why? It's just too bad, Corrie!'*

Self-pity creates darkness, and can even cause sickness. It is a very respectable sin, logical and convincing, and places self on the throne.

One evening all the neighbours turn up their radios. It is too much. No human being can bear this!

Suddenly I look into the mirror and burst out laughing. What a long face! How foolish to feel so sorry for myself. I try singing above the clamour, and sure enough, it works. The heat of the night can be endured, after all, for a prayer rises in my heart, 'Lord Jesus, You suffered so much to save me from sin and make me a child of Yours. Why shouldn't I endure a bit of discomfort in carrying Your message to others? You had no place to lay Your head. I have a bed, and a room, even though they are both filled with mosquitoes.'

A fortnight later a letter from Toronto reaches me. A friend writes, 'Today an acquaintance phoned and asked me if I knew you. She has never met you but has just finished reading your book AMAZING LOVE, and since then has been in prayer for you all day long. I asked her to visit me, and together we prayed for you.'

Is it not wonderful? How important is intercession! In Tokyo a child of God loses heart and falls into the sin of self-pity. Of course God can save her, but not until two of His children obey does He rescue Corrie ten Boom in Tokyo. (Not Good If Detached.)

7

Prayer Blessed be Jehovah God, the God of Israel, who only does wonderful things! Blessed be his glorious name forever! Let the whole earth be filled with his glory. Amen, and amen! (*Ps. 72:18, 19.*)

Promise The glory of the Lord will be seen by all mankind together. The Lord has spoken — it shall be. (*Is. 40:5.*)

8

Prayer O Lord, we have sinned against you grievously, yet help us for the sake of your own reputation! (*Jer. 14:7.*)

Promise I will cure you of idolatry and faithlessness, and my love will know no bounds. (*Hos. 14:4.*)

9

Prayer I *do* have faith; oh, help me to have *more*! (*Mark 9:24.*)

Promise If you had faith even as small as a tiny mustard seed you could say to this mountain, 'Move!' Nothing would be impossible. (*Matt. 17:20.*)

10

Prayer Scatter all who delight in war. (*Ps. 68:30.*)

Promise The Lord will settle international disputes; all the nations will convert their weapons of war into implements of peace. Then at the last all wars will stop and all military training will end. (*Is. 2:4.*)

11

Prayer Let the weak be strong. (*Joel 3:10.*)

Promise The people who know their God shall be strong and do great things. (*Dan. 11:32.*)

12

Prayer Help me. (*Ps. 119:86.*)

Promise Fear not, for I am with you. I am your God. I will strengthen you; I will help you; I will uphold you with my victorious right hand. (*Is. 41:10.*)

13

Prayer I am completely discouraged — I lie in the dust. Revive me by your Word. (*Ps. 119:25.*)

Promise He stoops to look, and lifts the poor from the dirt, and the hungry from the garbage dump. (*Ps. 113:7.*)

■ *When I was in a concentration camp during the last war, we had to stand every day for two or three hours for roll-call, often in the icy-cold wind. That was something terrible. Once a woman guard used these hours to demonstrate her cruelty. I could hardly bear to see and hear what happened in front of me. Suddenly a skylark started to sing high in the sky. We all looked up, and when I looked to the sky and listened to its song, I looked still higher and thought of Ps. 103:11 (RSV): 'For as the heavens are high above the earth, so great is his steadfast love toward those who fear him.' Suddenly I saw that this love of God was a greater reality than the cruelty that I experienced myself and saw around me. (Marching Orders.)*

14

Prayer Hallelujah! Thank you, Lord! How good you are! Your love for us continues on forever. (*Ps. 106:1.*)

Promise Nothing will ever be able to separate us from the love of God demonstrated by our Lord Jesus Christ when he died for us. (*Rom. 8:39.*)

15

Prayer   O Jehovah, God of Heaven's armies, how long will you be angry and reject our prayers ? (*Ps. 80: 4.*)

Promise   I will be quiet and not be angry with you anymore. (*Ezek. 16:42.*)

16

Prayer   Lord, you know how I long for my health once more. You hear my every sigh. (*Ps. 38:9.*)

Promise   I will give you back your health again and heal your wounds. (*Jer. 30:17.*)

17

Prayer   Now that I am old and grey, don't forsake me. Give me time to tell this new generation about all your mighty miracles. (*Ps. 71:18.*)

Promise   The godly shall flourish like palm trees and grow tall as the cedars of Lebanon. Even in old age they will still produce fruit and be vital and green. (*Ps. 92:12, 14.*)

18

Prayer   I am like an owl alone in the desert. I lie awake, lonely as a solitary sparrow on the roof. (*Ps. 102:6.*)

Promise   The Lord your God has arrived to live among you. He will rejoice over you in great gladness. He will love you. (*Zeph. 3:17, 18.*)

19

Prayer No man can live forever. All will die. Who can rescue his life from the power of the grave? (*Ps. 89:48.*)

Promise Our Saviour Jesus Christ ... broke the power of death and showed us the way of everlasting life through trusting him. (*2 Tim. 1:10.*)

20

Prayer Oh wash me, cleanse me from this guilt. Let me be pure again. (*Ps. 51:2.*)

Promise He is like a blazing fire refining precious metal and he can bleach the dirtiest garments! He will purify them like gold or silver, so that they will do their work for God with pure hearts. (*Mal. 3:2, 3.*)

■ *Today I have an especially fine interpreter. He loves the Lord with all his heart, and it is pure delight to work together — such a contrast to indifferent interpreters. Suddenly I ask, 'Why is there so much darkness in you?'*

'What do you mean?'

'There is no joy of the Lord in your eyes. In the parable of the vine and the branches, the Lord says, "That My joy might remain in you, and that your joy might be full." Where is that joy?'

'I don't know.'

'I think perhaps I know. May I speak? When you were converted from Shintoism to the Lord, you turned your back on demons, but the demons have not turned their backs on you.' In surprise he answers, 'That is true. But

please don't tell the missionaries. They may think I've gone back to Shintoism.'

'Demons are no ism. They are realities. You need not remain in darkness one moment longer. In the name of the Lord Jesus and by the blood of the Lamb we have the victory. In His name you can drive out the demons and withstand Satan.'

Together we read and obey the glorious promise and command in Mark 16:15–18, and then the Lord performs the miracle of the complete liberation of His child.

A few weeks later we meet again. 'Not only am I free,' he says, 'but my wife and children also.' All hail the power of Jesus' name! (Not Good If Detached.)

21

Prayer   I have wept until I am exhausted; my eyes are swollen with weeping, waiting for my God to act. (*Ps. 69:3.*)

Promise   Rest in the Lord; wait patiently for him to act. Trust him to help you and he will. (*Ps. 37:7, 5.*)

22

Prayer   Preserve my life from the conspiracy of these wicked men, these gangs of criminals. (*Ps. 64:2.*)

Promise   Jehovah himself is caring for you! He is your defender. He protects you day and night. He keeps you from all evil, and preserves your life. (*Ps. 121:5–7.*)

23

Prayer Never let it be said that God failed me. (*Ps. 119:116.*)

Promise We are able to hold our heads high no matter what happens and know that all is well, for we know how dearly God loves us. (*Rom. 5:5.*)

24

Prayer Do not hate us, Lord, for the sake of your own name. (*Jer. 14:21.*)

Promise I will live among you, and not despise you. (*Lev. 26:11.*)

25

Prayer Now hear me as I call again. Have mercy on me. Hear my prayer. (*Ps. 4:1.*)

Promise I want you to trust me in your times of trouble, so I can rescue you, and you can give me glory. (*Ps. 50:15.*)

26

Prayer Waken! Rouse yourself! Don't sleep, O Lord! . . . (*Ps. 44:23, 26.*)

Promise He will never let me stumble, slip or fall, for he is always watching, never sleeping. (*Ps. 121:3.*)

27

Prayer In your kindness spare my life; then I can continue to obey you. (*Ps. 119:88.*)

Promise I will refresh Israel like the dew from heaven; she will blossom as the lily. (*Hos. 14:5.*)

■ *In the cell of a prison a woman lies on her cot with a bored expression on her face. I feel such great love and compassion for this woman, and pray that the Lord will give me entrance to her heart.*

The ice is broken sooner than I expect, and we have a heart-to-heart talk. 'Do you sometimes make use of the time that you are alone to pray?' I ask.

'I don't know how to pray. Tell me something of your own prayer life.'

'For cakes you need ingredients, and you need them for prayer, too. For instance, the ingredients of a prayer could be: 1. The promises of God. 2. Our problems and needs. 3. Faith to bring these two together.' (Not Good If Detached.)

28

Prayer Teach the rest of us how we should approach God. For we are too dull to know! (*Job 37:19.*)
Promise The Holy Spirit helps us with our daily problems and in our praying . . . the Holy Spirit prays for us with such feeling that it cannot be expressed in words. (*Rom. 8:26.*)

29

Prayer Arm yourself, O Mighty One, so glorious, so majestic! And in your majesty, go on to victory. (*Ps. 45: 3, 4.*)
Promise The Lord our God, the Almighty, reigns. (*Rev. 19:6.*)

30

Prayer Pardon our iniquity and our sins. (*Ex. 34:9.*)
Promise In those days, says the Lord, no sin shall be found in Israel or in Judah, for I will pardon the remnant I preserve. (*Jer. 50:20.*)

31

Prayer Hear us, O Lord God, for we are being mocked. (*Neh. 4:4.*)
Promise These trials will make you partners with Christ in his suffering, and afterwards you will have the wonderful joy of sharing his glory in that coming day when it will be displayed. (*1 Pet. 4:13.*)

June

1

Prayer Let your constant love surround us, for our hopes are in you alone. (*Ps. 33:22.*)

Promise The loving-kindness of the Lord is from everlasting to everlasting, to those who reverence him. (*Ps. 103:17.*)

2

Prayer Don't disgrace me, Lord, by not replying when I call to you for aid. (*Ps. 31:17.*)

Promise You shall know that I am the Lord. Those who wait for me shall never be ashamed. (*Is. 49:23.*)

3

Prayer Teach me good judgment as well as knowledge. (*Ps. 119:66.*)

Promise He will teach the ways that are right and best to those who humbly turn to him. (*Ps. 25:9.*)

■ *I visited a prison in Ruanda. It was only a small building, but many prisoners were sitting outside on the ground.*

'*Where do you sleep at night?*' *I asked.*

'*Half of us sleep inside, the others must stay outside, because there are too many prisoners.*' *Some had a banana leaf, others had a branch or an old newspaper to sit on. It was all so sad. I prayed:* '*Lord, the fruit of the Spirit is joy. Give me an ocean of joy to share with these poor fellows.*' *He did what I asked. I could almost shout for joy. I told them of a friend whose name is Jesus, who is good and so full of love, who never leaves you alone.*

When I said goodbye, all the prisoners accompanied me to the car. '*What do they say?*' *I asked my interpreter. She laughed and said:* '*Old woman, come back, come back, and tell us more about Jesus.*' (*Marching Orders.*)

4

Prayer And now, in my old age, don't set me aside. Don't forsake me now when my strength is failing. (*Ps. 71:9.*)

Promise I will be your God through all your lifetime, yes, even when your hair is white with age. (*Is. 46:4.*)

5

Prayer Hide me in the shadow of your wings. (*Ps. 17:8.*)

Promise He will shield you with his wings! They will shelter you. (*Ps. 91:4.*)

6

Prayer Wash me and I shall be whiter than snow. (*Ps. 51:7.*)

Promise No matter how deep the stain of your sins, I can take it out and make you as clean as freshly fallen snow. Even if you are stained as red as crimson, I can make you white as wool! (*Is. 1:18.*)

7

Prayer Oh, send out your light and your truth — let them lead me. Let them lead me to your Temple on your holy mountain, Zion. (*Ps. 43:3.*)

Promise Your words are a flashlight to light the path ahead of me, and keep me from stumbling. (*Ps. 119:105.*)

8

Prayer O Lord my God, give me light in my darkness lest I die. (*Ps. 13:3.*)

Promise Jehovah God is our Light and our Protector. He gives grace and glory. (*Ps. 84:11.*)

9

Prayer Lord, waken! See what is happening! Help me! (*Ps. 59:4.*)

Promise He will never let me stumble, slip or fall. For he is always watching, never sleeping. (*Ps. 121:3, 4.*)

10

Prayer How can we know the way? (*John 14:5.*)

Promise I am the Way — yes, and the Truth and the Life. (*John 14:6.*)

■ *The uppermost tier of beds was built so close to the
ceiling that one could not sit upright on the beds. All about
me lay many young girls, courageous, sturdy girls. We had
been talking about guidance in our times. Now one of them
said:*

   '*It has certainly been no mistake that God directed my
life by way of Ravensbruck. Here, for the first time, I
have really learned to pray. The distress here has taught
me that things are never entirely right in one's life unless
he is completely surrendered to Jesus. I was always rather
pious, but there were areas in my life from which Jesus was
completely excluded. Now He is King in every sphere of
my life.*' (*A Prisoner And Yet.*)

11

Prayer   Give me back my joy again. (*Ps. 51:8.*)
Promise   The godly shall rejoice in the Lord, and
trust and praise him. (*Ps. 64:10.*)

12

Prayer   O God, in mercy bless us; let your face beam
with joy as you look down at us. (*Ps. 67:1.*)
Promise   When he sees all that is accomplished by
the anguish of his soul, he shall be satisfied. (*Is. 53:11.*)

13

Prayer   Help them [your people] to follow the good
ways in which they should walk. (*1 Kings 8:36.*)
Promise   I am the Lord your God, who punishes you
for your own good and leads you along the paths that
you should follow. (*Is. 48:17.*)

14

Prayer   Rescue me, O God, from my poverty and pain. (*Ps. 69:29.*)

Promise   The rocks of the mountains will be their fortress of safety; food will be supplied to them and they will have all the water they need. (*Is. 33:16.*)

15

Prayer   Oh, have mercy on us and do something if you can. (*Mark 9:22.*)

Promise   I will return and have compassion on all of you. (*Jer. 12:15.*)

16

Prayer   Let your priests, O Lord God, be clothed with salvation, and let your saints rejoice in your kind deeds. (*2 Chron. 6:41.*)

Promise   I will clothe her priests with salvation; her saints shall shout for joy. (*Ps. 132:16.*)

17

Prayer   Honour your name by leading me. (*Ps. 31:3.*)

Promise   The Lord will guide you continually. (*Is. 58:11.*)

■ *It was during a visit to [a] friend that she asked me if I could arrange to go to Bermuda for a week. As far as time was concerned, it was possible to add it to my schedule. But I did not have money for the plane trip. So I asked the Lord for guidance. When it became clear that He wanted me to go, I wrote immediately to Bermuda saying that I would come; the matter of money I entrusted to the Lord. Within two or three days, cheques arrived from different people, people who knew nothing of the proposed trip. And there was just enough money for a return ticket. (Amazing Love.)*

18

Prayer Don't leave me, Lord; don't go away! Come quickly! Help me, O my Saviour. (*Ps. 38:21, 22.*)

Promise What a wonderful God we have — he is the Father of our Lord Jesus Christ, the source of every mercy, and the one who wonderfully comforts and strengthens us in our hardships and trials. (*2 Cor. 1:3, 4.*)

19

Prayer When my heart is faint and overwhelmed, lead me to the mighty, towering Rock of safety. (*Ps. 61: 2.*)

Promise Jehovah is my rock, my fortress and my Saviour. He is my shield and my salvation, my refuge and high tower. (*2 Sam. 22:2, 3.*)

20

Prayer Let your tenderhearted mercies meet our needs. (*Ps. 79:8.*)

Promise Through Christ, all the kindness of God has been poured out upon us. (*Rom. 1:5.*)

Prayer I will not let you go until you bless me.
(*Gen. 32:26.*)
Promise I will bless you with incredible blessings.
(*Gen. 22:17.*)

22

Prayer Point out anything you find in me that makes
you sad, and lead me along the path of everlasting life.
(*Ps. 139:24.*)
Promise My paths are those of justice and right.
(*Prov. 8:20.*)

23

Prayer Look down from your holy home in heaven
and bless your people. (*Deut. 26:15.*)
Promise He will surely bless us. He will bless the
people of Israel. (*Ps. 115:12.*)

24

Prayer Lord, you alone can heal me. (*Jer. 17:14.*)
Promise I will heal him. (*2 Kings 20:5.*)

■ *Some time ago in San Diego, I met a man who told a
story of the power of intercessory prayer. He had been a
heavy drinker, and was finally taken to a psychopathic
hospital. Here he was placed in a room with three other
patients, who did nothing but scream. When night came he
was in despair. He prayed, but could not fall asleep while*

the screams continued. Then suddenly he began to pray for the three patients, and just as suddenly the screams ceased.

'Not only that,' continued the man, 'it seemed as if something broke in me. When I prayed for others, my own tension was released, and I was free. The next day I had to undergo a psychiatric examination. At its conclusion the doctor said, "There is nothing wrong with you; you are normal." I knew that night that I had become a free man.'

Intercession often adds to its many other blessings the healing of one's own tension. (Amazing Love.)

25

Prayer I will try to walk a blameless path, but how I need your help! (*Ps. 101:2.*)
Promise He is able to keep you from slipping and falling away. (*Jude 1:24.*)

26

Prayer Rescue the poor and needy from the grasp of evil men. (*Ps. 82:4.*)
Promise He stands beside the poor and hungry to save them from their enemies. (*Ps. 109:31.*)

27

Prayer Because of all your faithful mercies, Lord, please turn away your furious anger. (*Dan. 9:16.*)
Promise My anger will be forever gone! (*Hos. 14:4.*)

28

Prayer Bend low, O Lord, and listen. Open your eyes, O Lord, and see. (*2 Kings 19:16.*)

Promise The eyes of the Lord are intently watching all who live good lives, and he gives attention when they cry to him. (*Ps. 34:15.*)

29

Prayer When will you comfort me with your help? (*Ps. 119:82.*)

Promise I will comfort you there as a little one is comforted by its mother. (*Is. 66:13.*)

30

Prayer Oh, for wings like a dove, to fly away and rest! (*Ps. 55:6.*)

Promise Come to me and I will give you rest — all you who work so hard beneath a heavy yoke. (*Matt. 11: 28.*)

July

1

Prayer O Jehovah, why have you thrown my life away? Why are you turning your face from me, and looking the other way? (*Ps. 88:14.*)

Promise In a moment of anger I turned my face a little while; but with everlasting love I will have pity on you, says the Lord, your Redeemer. (*Is. 54:8.*)

▆ *One day news reached us that a young woman in hospital Barracks 8 had lost courage completely. We decided to make an effort to get through to her somehow. Visiting in the hospital was strictly forbidden. But five of us went over there. In a corner near the barracks we held a simple prayer meeting. Then I set out. I knew which window was nearest her bed, but saw at once that the shutters were closed.*

I went back and we prayed together: 'Lord, wilt Thou cause the shutters to be opened?' A Lagerpolizei passed the barracks and opened the shutters. Again I went over and stood next to her window, but now there was a new difficulty — the window could not be opened from the out-

67

side. So once more I went back to my friends and we prayed together that the window might be opened. Before I got back a Polish woman had opened the window from the inside. (A Prisoner And Yet.)

2

Prayer Please, Lord, rescue me! Quick! Come and help me! (*Ps. 40:13.*)

Promise The Lord says, 'Because he loves me, I will rescue him.' (*Ps. 91:14.*)

3

Prayer Sir, help me! (*Matt. 15:25.*)

Promise Despised though you are, fear not, O Israel; for I will help you. (*Is. 41:14.*)

4

Prayer O Lord God, don't destroy your own people. (*Deut. 9:25.*)

Promise The Lord will not forsake his people. (*Ps. 94:14.*)

5

Prayer Rescue me from my persecutors, for they are too strong for me. (*Ps. 142:6.*)

Promise The Angel of the Lord guards and rescues all who reverence him. (*Ps. 34:7.*)

6

Prayer Restore to me again the joy of your salvation, and make me willing to obey you. (*Ps. 51:12.*)

Promise When the Holy Spirit controls our lives he will produce this kind of fruit in us: love, joy. . . . (*Gal. 5:22.*)

7

Prayer O Jehovah, come and bless us! How long will you delay? (*Ps. 90:13.*)

Promise Jehovah will vindicate his people, and have compassion on his servants. (*Ps. 135:14.*)

8

Prayer Prove them wrong, O Lord, by letting the light of your face shine down upon us. (*Ps. 4:6.*)

Promise May the Lord's face radiate with joy because of you; may he be gracious to you. (*Num. 6: 26.*)

Betsie stood leaning against me; my arms were thrown about her. It was one of the few times when she observed and was vulnerable to the misery around her. Softly she whispered, 'Oh, Corrie, this is hell.'

'God has promised, "I will never leave thee nor forsake thee",' I whispered back.

The sky suddenly reddened. The sun had not yet risen, but the clouds, driven before the wind, caught its rays from beneath the horizon, and reflected a ruddy glow on the earth. Even dark clouds, illuminated by the sun, spread light and colour over everything. 'So will the light from our Saviour shine on us here in Ravensbruck, and we shall reflect its colour and glow,' I said softly. (*A Prisoner And Yet.*)

9

Prayer   Remember how short you have made man's lifespan. (*Ps. 89:47.*)

Promise   He knows we are but dust, and that our days are few and brief. (*Ps. 103:14.*)

10

Prayer   Rescue me from the oppression of evil men. (*Ps. 119:134.*)

Promise   Your enemies will stay far away; you will live in peace. Terror shall not come near. (*Is. 54:14.*)

11

Prayer   O Lord, deliver me from evil men. Preserve me from the violent. (*Ps. 140:1.*)

Promise   He keeps his eye upon you as you come and go, and always guards you. (*Ps. 121:8.*)

12

Prayer   You have seen me tossing and turning through the night. You have collected all my tears and preserved them in your bottle! (*Ps. 56:8.*)

Promise   I will lie down in peace and sleep, for though I am alone, O Lord, you will keep me safe. (*Ps. 4:8.*)

13

Prayer Make me walk along the right paths for I know how delightful they really are. (*Ps. 119:35.*)

Promise I will put my Spirit within you so that you will obey my laws and do whatever I command. (*Ezek. 36:27.*)

14

Prayer I look to you for help, O Lord God. You are my refuge. Don't let them slay me. (*Ps. 141:8.*)

Promise He will listen to the prayers of the destitute, for he is never too busy to heed their requests. (*Ps. 102:17.*)

15

Prayer O Lord, don't punish me while you are angry! (*Ps. 38:1.*)

Promise I swear that I will never again pour out my anger on you. (*Is. 54:9.*)

■ *'Today you will address one hundred and forty gang-sters,' the warder warns me. There they sit closely-packed on the floor, long rows of Japanese sitting on their heels. My first reaction is, 'What darkness!' Cruel faces stare at me.*

The lost ones! The world has only one answer, to keep them behind barbed wire. Then great joy arises in my heart. I have a message for them; the answer to their prob-lems. An ocean of sin and darkness was covered with a greater ocean of love and light when Jesus died upon the cross. It was for them He died and bore the sins of the whole world.

I tell them of this ocean of love. 'Your souls are precious in the sight of God. Accept Jesus as your Lord and Saviour and He will give you power to become children of God. The tender father-heart of God yearns for your love.'

I can almost see the faces change. I see God's love at work, and His love overflows in my heart as never before. What great riches! The prisoners applaud. It is the only expression allowed them, and their applause is long and loud. (*Not Good If Detached.*)

16

Prayer Don't hide from me, for I am in deep trouble. Quick! Come and save me. (*Ps. 69:17.*)
Promise Here on earth you will have many trials and sorrows; but cheer up, for I have overcome the world. (*John 16:33.*)

17

Prayer God of Israel, arise and punish the heathen nations surrounding us. (*Ps. 59:5.*)
Promise Thus I will demonstrate my glory among the nations; all shall see the punishment of God and know that I have done it. (*Ezek. 39:21.*)

18

Prayer Cross-examine me, O Lord, and see that this is so; test my motives and affections too. (*Ps. 26:2.*)
Promise You, the righteous God, look deep within the hearts of men and examine all their motives and their thoughts. (*Ps. 7:9.*)

19

Prayer Cleanse me from these hidden faults. (*Ps. 19: 12.*)

Promise I will take from you your hearts of stone and give you tender hearts of love for God. (*Ezek. 11: 19.*)

20

Prayer O Lord my God, you have heard and answered my request. (*1 Kings 8:28.*)

Promise Though he is so great, he respects the humble. (*Ps. 138:6.*)

21

Prayer O Lord God of our fathers — the only God in all the heavens, the Ruler of all the kingdoms of the earth — you are so powerful, so mighty. (*2 Chron. 20:6.*)

Promise I shall be your God and the God of your posterity. (*Gen. 17:7.*)

22

Prayer O Lord, have mercy on me in my anguish. My eyes are red from weeping. (*Ps. 31:9.*)

Promise The Lord has comforted his people, and will have compassion upon them in their sorrow. (*Is. 49:13.*)

■ *We were lined up in the hospital corridor for medical inspection. We had to remove all our clothes and lay them on the floor of the entrance hall. Never in my life had I felt so wretched, so cold, or so humiliated.*

Suddenly I recalled a painting of Jesus on Golgotha. For the first time I realised that Jesus had hung naked upon the cross. How he must have suffered! He, God's Son, whose home was Heaven! And all that suffering He bore for me, that I might some day go to Heaven.

My soul became calm within me. I felt that strength was given me to go on. I prayed, 'O Saviour, Thou didst suffer for me on Calvary. I thank Thee for it. Help me now to bear this present experience. Give me strength!' (A Prisoner And Yet.)

23

Prayer Show me the path where I should go, O Lord; point out the right road for me to walk. (*Ps. 25: 4.*)

Promise He will tell us what to do and we will do it. (*Mic. 4:2.*)

24

Prayer Bless your chosen ones. Lead them like a shepherd and carry them forever in your arms. (*Ps. 28: 9.*)

Promise Trust in the Lord . . . Be kind and good to others; then you will live safely here in the land and prosper, feeding in safety. (*Ps. 37:3.*)

25

Prayer Open up, O heavens. Let the skies pour out their righteousness. (*Is. 45:8.*)

Promise Truth rises from the earth and righteousness smiles down from heaven. (*Ps. 85:11.*)

26

Prayer   Don't allow us to be tempted. (*Luke 11:4.*)
Promise   I will protect you from the time of Great Tribulation and temptation. (*Rev. 3:10.*)

27

Prayer   Protect me from death, for I try to follow all your laws. Save me, for I am serving you and trusting you. (*Ps. 86:2.*)
Promise   He keeps you from all evil, and preserves your life. (*Ps. 121:7.*)

28

Prayer   Let me share in your chosen ones' prosperity and rejoice in all their joys, and receive the glory you give to them. (*Ps. 106:5.*)
Promise   May the Lord continually bless you with heaven's blessings as well as with human joys. May you live to enjoy your grandchildren! And may God bless Israel! (*Ps. 128:5, 6.*)

29

Prayer   O God, have pity, for I am trusting you! I will hide beneath the shadow of your wings until this storm is past. (*Ps. 57:1.*)
Promise   Jehovah himself is caring for you! He is your defender. (*Ps. 121:5.*)

■ *Praying is bringing to the Lord everything that troubles and distresses us. It means leaving our burden of cares with Him and going on without it. That day I had been very stupid: I had gathered up all my cares, and after prayer the burden had seemed twice as heavy as it had before. And so I prayed, 'Lord teach me to cast all my burdens upon Thee and go on without them. Only Thy Spirit can teach me that lesson. Give me Thy Spirit, O Lord, and I shall have faith, such faith that I shall no longer carry a load of care.'* (*A Prisoner And Yet.*)

30

Prayer   Keep me far from every wrong; help me, undeserving as I am, to obey your laws. (*Ps. 119:29.*)
Promise   I will write my laws in their minds so that they will know what I want them to do without my even telling them, and these laws will be in their hearts so that they will want to obey them, and I will be their God and they shall be my people. (*Heb. 8:10.*)

31

Prayer   End all wickedness, O Lord, and bless all who truly worship God. (*Ps. 7:9.*)
Promise   All nations will come and worship before you. (*Rev. 15:4.*)

August

1

Prayer   Give me some of that water! Then I'll never be thirsty again. (*John 4:15.*)

Promise   I will give to the thirsty the springs of the Water of Life. (*Rev. 21:6.*)

2

Prayer   Give fair judgment to the poor man, the afflicted, the fatherless, the destitute. (*Ps. 82:3.*)

Promise   He has appointed me to preach Good News to the poor; he has sent me to heal the brokenhearted and to announce ... that the downtrodden shall be freed from their oppressors. (*Luke 4:18.*)

3

Prayer   We will worship you and you alone if you will only rescue us from our enemies. (*1 Sam. 12:10.*)

Promise   You must worship only the Lord; he will save you from all your enemies. (*2 Kings 17:39.*)

Prayer You will keep on guiding me all my life with your wisdom and counsel; and afterwards receive me into the glories of heaven! (*Ps. 73:24.*)

Promise For this great God is our God forever and ever. He will be our guide until we die. (*Ps. 48:14.*)

5

Prayer Give me sense to heed your laws. (*Ps. 119: 73.*)

Promise Where is the man who fears the Lord? God will teach him how to choose the best. (*Ps. 25:12.*)

■ *I was attending a meeting of students in the State of Washington on the west coast of the United States. One of them said, 'I said "yes" to the Lord many years ago; what do you suppose is the reason that I've retrogressed so much since then? I sometimes doubt that I meant it seriously at the time.'*

A tall medical student answered him: 'Once there was a boy who fell out of bed. His mother asked him how he happened to do that, and he answered, "Mummy, it happened because I fell asleep too close to the place where I climbed in." That is also what happens to many Christians. When they are converted they think that they have reached the goal. When one is converted, and says "yes" to Jesus, it does not mean the end of a new experience, but the beginning of it. To enter the Kingdom of Heaven through the gate of conversion means to enter into a world of riches. All the promises in the Bible become your property. You have to find out what it means "For all the promises of God in Him are yea, and in Him Amen" (II Cor. 1:20). You have to find out how rich you are.' (Amazing Love.)

6

Prayer Oh, don't forsake me and let me slip back into sin again. (*Ps. 119:8.*)

Promise He is able to keep you from slipping and falling away, and to bring you, sinless and perfect, into his glorious presence with mighty shouts of everlasting joy. (*Jude 1:24.*)

7

Prayer Rouse yourself and use your mighty power to rescue us. (*Ps. 80:2.*)

Promise You will save those in trouble. (*2 Sam. 22: 28.*)

8

Prayer Lord, you know my heart; you know I am [your friend]. (*John 21:17.*)

Promise The one who obeys me is the one who loves me, and because he loves me, my Father will love him; and I will too, and I will reveal myself to him. (*John 14:21.*)

9

Prayer Surely you won't be angry about such a little thing! Surely you will just forget it? (*Jer. 3:5.*)

Promise I am merciful; I will not be forever angry with you. Only acknowledge your guilt. (*Jer. 3:12.*)

10

Prayer See my sorrows; feel my pain; forgive my sins. (*Ps. 25:18.*)

Promise Cheer up, son! For I have forgiven your sins! (*Matt. 5:2.*)

11

Prayer Oh, revive us! Then your people can rejoice in you again. (*Ps. 85:6.*)

Promise I refresh the humble and give new courage to those with repentant hearts. (*Is. 57:15.*)

12

Prayer Give me light in my darkness lest I die. (*Ps. 13:3.*)

Promise The Lord My God has made my darkness turn to light. (*Ps. 18:28.*)

May and I were taking a walk along the cliffs. We had heard the day before an impressive lecture on unconditional surrender to God. May used the time to scoff at the lecture. I looked at her, and couldn't help smiling.

'I would like to surrender to Jesus,' she said. 'Actually I know the way, but when I am on the point of saying "yes" a barrier seems to arise and keep me from surrendering.'

'Listen, May. Think back over the events of your life and tell me if you have ever been in touch with spiritism. Have you ever been to a fortune-teller? Do you know that when you do such a thing you fall under the spell of it, through which the way to God becomes barred for you?'

May laughed in a mocking way. 'As a matter of fact, I did go to a fortune-teller years ago,' she said, 'but I did not believe in it. I did it only for fun.'

'May, suppose you were a soldier during a war. By mistake you fell into the enemy's hands by entering his territory. Do you think that it would help if you then said, "Oh, excuse me, please, it was not my intention to come here; I just came by mistake?" Once you are on their terrain, you are at their mercy. Though you did not know it, a demon has taken possession of your heart, and your life has fallen under his spell. When you want to be converted he comes in between. St. Paul says in Ephesians 6: 12, "For we wrestle not against flesh and blood, but against principalities, against powers." ' The look of amusement had left May's face, and fear was there instead.

'I'm not telling you these things to make you afraid, May. The wonderful thing about it is that Jesus is the victor. He is far stronger than all the powers of hell. Ask the Lord Jesus to go back with you to that very moment when you committed that sin. Confess your sin, ask forgiveness, and give thanks for it. Then the door is closed and you are free. Will you do it, May? I'll leave you to yourself now.'

On the last night of the conference the leader asked if any would tell what they had learned and experienced these weeks. May stood up and said, 'I have learned and experienced here that Jesus is victor.' (Amazing Love.)

13

Prayer Search me, O God, and know my heart; test my thought. Point out anything you find in me that makes you sad, and lead me along the path of everlasting life. (*Ps. 139:23, 24.*)

Promise Whatever God says to us is full of living power: it is sharper than the sharpest dagger, cutting swift and deep into our innermost thoughts and desires with all their parts, exposing us for what we really are. (*Heb. 4:12.*)

14

Prayer If you want to, you can heal me. (*Matt. 8:2.*)

Promise 'I want to,' [Jesus] says; 'be healed.' (*Matt. 8:3.*)

15

Prayer You have seen the wrong they did to me; be my judge, to prove me right. (*Lam. 3:59.*)

Promise The Lord will surely help those they persecute; he will maintain the rights of the poor. (*Ps. 140: 12.*)

16

Prayer Send me a sign of your favour. When those who hate me see it they will lose face because you help and comfort me. (*Ps. 86:17.*)

Promise Friendship with God is reserved for those who reverence him. With them alone he shares the secrets of his promises. (*Ps. 25:14.*)

17

Prayer Help us for the honour of your name. Oh, save us and forgive our sins. (*Ps. 79:9.*)
Promise I will cleanse away your sins. (*Ezek. 36:29.*)

18

Prayer Spare your people, O our God. (*Joel 2:17.*)
Promise I will spare them as a man spares an obedient and dutiful son. (*Mal. 3:17.*)

19

Prayer If you are planning to make my mission a success, please guide me in this way. (*Gen. 24:42.*)
Promise My Lord, in whose presence I have walked, will send his angel with you and make your mission successful. (*Gen. 24:40.*)

■ *Tomorrow I must make a short trip and pay the rent for my room. It is not a large sum I need, but it just is not there. Those very fine, helpful friends, shall I ask them? 'May I not tell them, Father, that I need the money?' I pray. But the answer is plain. 'Trust Me.'*

It is a busy day: three meetings and several talks with people. Tired out, I return to my room. My mail has come, twenty-six letters, the first to arrive in Formosa. There is not time to read them all now, but out of the first one I open falls a cheque for £50! (Not Good If Detached.)

20

Prayer   O God, my God! How I search for you! How I thirst for you in this parched and weary land where there is no water. How I long to find you! How I wish I could go into your sanctuary to see your strength and glory. (*Ps. 63:1, 2.*)

Promise   I will bring them also to my holy mountain of Jerusalem, and make them full of joy within my House of Prayer. (*Is. 56:7.*)

21

Prayer   Save me from being overpowered by my sins. (*Ps. 39:8.*)

Promise   No temptation is irresistible. He will show you how to escape temptation's power so that you can bear up patiently against it. (*1 Cor. 10:13.*)

22

Prayer   Help your people and protect Jerusalem. (*Ps. 51:18.*)

Promise   God will save Jerusalem; he rebuilds the cities of Judah. (*Ps. 69:35.*)

23

Prayer   Come with great power, O God, and save me! Defend me with your might! (*Ps. 54:1.*)

Promise   The Lord is our Judge, our Lawgiver and our King; he will care for us and save us. (*Is. 33:22.*)

24

Prayer O God, my God! How I search for you! (*Ps. 63:1.*)

Promise Those who search for me shall surely find me. (*Prov. 8:17.*)

25

Prayer O God, don't hide yourself when I cry to you. Hear me, Lord! Listen to me! (*Ps. 55:1, 2.*)

Promise When you call, the Lord will answer. 'Yes, I am here,' he will quickly reply. (*Is. 58:9.*)

26

Prayer Yes, Lord, help us against our enemies, for man's help is useless. (*Ps. 60:11.*)

Promise In your day of trouble, may the Lord be with you! May the God of Jacob keep you from all harm. May he send you aid from his sanctuary in Zion. (*Ps. 20:1, 2.*)

■ *A great gate led into the camp of Ravensbruck. The gate opened, and we marched in past the guards.*

As evening fell, some of the women lay down on the ground. Betsie and I remained standing; but then it suddenly dawned on us that we were to spend the night here. We were to sleep out under the open sky. We lay down close together and drew our blanket over us. 'He giveth His beloved sleep,' said Betsie. I looked up at the stars above us. He who held the stars in their orbits would not leave us alone. 'The night is dark, and I am far from home, lead Thou me on.' And then we fell asleep. (A Prisoner And Yet.)

Prayer   Ransom Israel from all her troubles. (*Ps. 25:22.*)

Promise   In all their affliction he was afflicted, and he personally saved them. (*Is. 63:9.*)

28

Prayer   I am in trouble — help me. (*Is. 38:14.*)

Promise   I will arise and defend the oppressed, the poor, the needy. I will rescue them as they have longed for me to do. (*Ps. 12:5.*)

29

Prayer   Into your hand I commit my spirit. You have rescued me, O God who keeps his promises. (*Ps. 31:5.*)

Promise   I am ... the Living One who died, who is now alive forevermore, who has the keys of hell and death — don't be afraid! (*Rev. 1:18.*)

30

Prayer   Be for me a great Rock of safety from my foes. (*Ps. 31:2.*)

Promise   He will shelter Israel from the storm and wind. He will refresh her as a river in the desert and as the cooling shadow of a mighty rock within a hot and weary land. (*Is. 32:2.*)

31

Prayer And now, Lord God, do as you have promised concerning me and my family. (*2 Sam. 7:25.*)

Promise The loving-kindness of the Lord is from everlasting to everlasting, to those who reverence him; his salvation is to children's children of those who are faithful to his covenant and remember to obey him! (*Ps. 103:17, 18.*)

September

1

Prayer Lord, teach us a prayer to recite just as John taught one of his disciples. (*Luke 11:1*.)

Promise I will pour out the spirit of grace and prayer on all the people of Jerusalem. (*Zech. 12:10*.)

2

Prayer Save me from my enemies, O Lord, I run to you to hide me. (*Ps. 142:9*.)

Promise The Lord is a strong fortress. The godly run to him and are safe. (*Prov. 18:10*.)

■ *One day I was permitted to join a 'team' that worked regularly in a large prison. One of the women opened the service by singing to the accompaniment of the organ. She sang in a very affected manner, and the response was anything but favourable. At both ends of the corridor the prisoners began shrieking, yelling, and screaming to drown the voice of the singer. Then one of the young men with us began to pray, speaking in a very unctuous manner. The effect was even worse. The prisoners had found a pail and were rolling it back and forth over the floor. The din was*

*terrific. 'Lord, must I speak in this place? I cannot.' I
prayed in desperation.*

*'Be not afraid; only believe. You can do all things
through Him who strengthens you. There will be a great
victory,' said the Lord to me. (Amazing Love.)*

3

Prayer Let your loving-kindness comfort me. (*Ps.
119:76.*)

Promise He loves us very dearly. (*Ps. 117:2.*)

4

Prayer Be gracious, Lord, and make me well again.
(*Ps. 41:10.*)

Promise Their prayer, if offered in faith, will heal
him, for the Lord will make him well; and if his sickness was caused by some sin, the Lord will forgive him.
(*James 5:15.*)

5

Prayer Lead me in good paths, for your Spirit is
good. (*Ps. 143:10.*)

Promise The Lord will guide you continually, and
satisfy you with all good things. (*Is. 58:11.*)

6

Prayer Don't fail me, Lord, for I am trusting you.
(*Ps. 25:2.*)

Promise Those who believe in him will never be
disappointed. (*Rom. 9:33.*)

7

Prayer Help me, O Lord my God! Save me because you are loving and kind. (*Ps. 109:26.*)

Promise He is a mighty saviour. He will give you victory. He will rejoice over you in great gladness. (*Zeph. 3:17.*)

8

Prayer Will you stand silent and still punish us? (*Is. 64:12.*)

Promise He does not enjoy afflicting men and causing sorrow. (*Lam. 3:33.*)

9

Prayer Act now and rescue me. (*Ps. 35:17.*)

Promise He feels pity for the weak and needy, and will rescue them. (*Ps. 72:13.*)

■ *A sick woman sits in a dirty, messy little kitchen. There is hardly room for my stool. I am eager for a quiet talk with her because she has twice called on a fortune-teller who claimed magic healing power. I tell her what a great sin this is in God's sight, because it really means that we run away from God and ask the devil for help. A great compassion comes into my heart for this woman. I tell her about the longing father-heart of God who loves us so much. I read to her what Jesus says: 'Come unto Me, all ye that labour and are heavy laden, and I will give you rest.' (Matt. 11:28). Before I leave she prays. She asks forgiveness for going to the fortune-teller, and then she praises and thanks God for the great riches she has in Jesus Christ. (Not Good If Detached.)*

10

Prayer   I trust in your salvation Lord. (*Gen. 49:18.*)
Promise   I give them eternal life and they shall never perish. (*John 10:28.*)

11

Prayer   Pull me out of this mire. Don't let me sink in. Rescue me from those who hate me, and from these deep waters I am in. (*Ps. 69:14.*)
Promise   Don't be afraid, for I have ransomed you; I have called you by name; you are mine. When you go through deep waters and great trouble, I will be with you. When you go through rivers of difficulty, you will not drown! (*Is. 43:1, 2.*)

12

Prayer   Arise, O Lord! Save me, O my God! (*Ps. 3: 7.*)
Promise   I am with you and I will save you, says the Lord. (*Jer. 30:11.*)

13

Prayer   Hear my prayer, O Lord; answer my plea. (*Ps. 143:11.*)
Promise   Listen to me! You can pray for *anything*, and *if you believe, you have it*; it's yours! (*Mark 12:24.*)

14

Prayer It is a broken spirit you want — remorse and penitence. (*Ps. 51:17.*)

Promise The high and lofty one who inhabits eternity, the Holy One, says this: I live in that high and holy place where those with contrite, humble spirits dwell. (*Is. 57:15.*)

15

Prayer O God enthroned in heaven, I lift my eyes to you. (*Ps. 123:1.*)

Promise Your eyes will see the King in his beauty. (*Is. 33:17.*)

16

Prayer To us, O Lord, be merciful, for we have waited for you. (*Is. 33:2.*)

Promise The Lord still waits for you to come to him, so he can show you his love ... blessed are all those who wait for him. (*Is. 30:18.*)

We heard one hundred and eighty shots. Every shot meant the death of a good Netherlander. That we knew. I laid my head on Betsie's shoulder. Could misery become so great that one would collapse under it?

I spoke now to the Lord. 'Thou hast borne all our griefs, O Lord. Wilt Thou not also bear this one?'

'Yes, my child, and you yourself need not, and cannot, and may not bear the sorrows of the world about you.'

I went with Betsie to the barracks, and a bit later was lying beside her in bed. I did not sleep, but rested quietly and there was peace in my heart. God makes no mistakes. Everything looks like a confused piece of embroidery work, meaningless and ugly. But that is the underside. Some day we shall see the right side and shall be amazed and thankful. (A Prisoner And Yet.)

17

Prayer   O Hope of Israel, our Saviour in times of trouble, . . . don't desert us now! (*Jer. 14:8, 9.*)
Promise   I will not abandon you or leave you as orphans in the storm — I will come to you. (*John 14: 18.*)

18

Prayer   Assign me Godliness and Integrity as my bodyguards. (*Ps. 25:21.*)
Promise   Good men will be rescued from harm. (*Prov. 28:18.*)

19

Prayer   Come, Lord, and rescue me. Ransom me from all my enemies. (*Ps. 69:18.*)
Promise   When you draw close to God, God will draw close to you. (*James 4:8.*)

20

Prayer   Yes, O my God, be wide awake and attentive to all the prayers made to you in this place. (*2 Chron. 6: 40.*)
Promise   I will listen, wide awake, to every prayer made in this place. (*2 Chron. 7:15.*)

Prayer O my God, save me from my enemies. (*Ps. 59:1.*)

Promise I, the Lord, will be with you and see you through. (*Jer. 1:8.*)

Prayer May the Lord our God be with us as he was with our fathers; may he never forsake us. (*1 Kings 8: 57.*)

Promise The Lord will not abandon his chosen people, for that would dishonour his great name. He made you a special nation for himself — just because he wanted to! (*1 Sam. 12:22.*)

Prayer Please help me now. (*Neh. 1:11.*)

Promise The God of heaven will help us. (*Neh. 2: 20.*)

■ *I once travelled by car through the mountains of California from Los Angeles to San Francisco. Along one side of the road was a deep chasm, and moreover, there were many dangerous curves. I knew from experience what to do when the demon of fear entered my heart. He had called on me many a time during my imprisonment in Germany, and I would then begin to sing. Singing always helps.*

So I sang one hymn after another, until my host, the driver, said teasingly, 'Are you afraid?'

'Yes,' I said, 'that is why I am singing.'

But this time it was all to no avail. Every time we

approached a curve, I would think, 'If another car is coming towards us from beyond that curve, we shall certainly crash into each other!' And, thoroughly frightened, I would stop singing.

Then I tried to dispel my fear by prayer, and I prayed. But my prayer became a refrain: 'Lord, bring us safely to San Francisco. Do not let us crash down into this abyss.'

I kept on praying to dispel my fear, until suddenly, and I do not know how the idea came to me, I began to pray for others. I prayed for everyone who came into my thoughts, people with whom I had travelled, those who had been in prison with me, my school friends of years ago. I do not know how long I continued in prayer, but this I do know, my fear was gone. Interceding for others had released me. (Amazing Love.)

24

Prayer Protect me from these who have come to destroy me. (*Ps. 59:1.*)
Promise I am with you and no one can harm you. (*Acts 18:10.*)

25

Prayer Oh, do not hide yourself when I am trying to find you. Do not angrily reject your servant. (*Ps. 27:9.*)
Promise I have loved you, O my people, with an everlasting love. (*Jer. 31:3.*)

26

Prayer   Oh, that I knew where to find God — that I could go to his throne and talk with him there. (*Job 23: 3.*)

Promise   You will find me when you seek me, if you look for me in earnest. (*Jer. 29:13.*)

27

Prayer   Oh, wash me, cleanse me from this guilt. Let me be pure again. (*Ps. 51:2.*)

Promise   It will be as though I had sprinkled clean water on you, for you will be clean — your filthiness will be washed away. (*Ezek. 36:25.*)

28

Prayer   Why not just pardon my sin and take it all away? (*Job 7:21.*)

Promise   Let them turn to the Lord that he may have mercy upon them, and to our God, for he will abundantly pardon! (*Is. 55:7.*)

29

Prayer   May every fibre of my being unite in reverence to your name. (*Ps. 86:11.*)

Promise   I will put a desire in their hearts to worship me. (*Jer. 32:40.*)

Prayer O Lord, deal with me as your child, as one who bears your name! Because you are so kind, O Lord, deliver me. (*Ps. 109:21.*)

Promise When the poor and needy seek water and there is none and their tongues are parched from thirst, then I will answer when they cry to me. I, Israel's God, will not ever forsake them. (*Is. 41:17.*)

■ '*O Lord, please have them give me a little of that toasted bread.' Immediately afterwards they passed me the plate, and I bit into the 'tasty tart.' How very delicious it was! But there was shame in my heart. Was I becoming egoistic and covetous? Was hunger going to get me down? A few minutes later, before eating our turnip soup, I prayed: 'Lord, bless this food for Jesus' sake, Amen.'*

How often I had prayed those words thoughtlessly! Now they were fraught with meaning. If God's blessing rested on this food it would be enough, and it would also keep me from becoming covetous. (A Prisoner And Yet).

October

1

Prayer   Just tell me what to do and I will do it, Lord. As long as I live I'll wholeheartedly obey. (*Ps. 119:33.*)
Promise   The Lord is good and glad to teach the proper path to all who go astray. (*Ps. 25:8.*)

2

Prayer   Protect me as you would the pupil of your eye. (*Ps. 17:8.*)
Promise   I am with you, and will protect you wherever you go. (*Gen. 28:15.*)

3

Prayer   Rescue me from death; spare my precious life from all these evil men. Save me from these lions' jaws. (*Ps. 22:20, 21.*)
Promise   The God of peace will soon crush Satan under your feet. (*Rom. 16:20.*)

4

Prayer Has his steadfast love forever ceased? Are his promises at an end for all time? (*Ps. 77:8.*)

Promise He [Jesus] carries out and fulfils all of God's promises, no matter how many of them there are. (*2 Cor. 1:20.*)

5

Prayer Don't let these proud men trample me. (*Ps. 36:11.*)

Promise God gives strength to the humble, but sets himself against the proud and haughty. (*James 4:6.*)

6

Prayer Let us see your miracles again; let our children see glorious things. (*Ps. 90:16.*)

Promise Anyone believing in me shall do the same miracles I have done, and even greater ones, because I am going to be with the Father. (*John 14:12.*)

7

Prayer Turn us again to yourself, O God. Look down on us in joy and love; only then shall we be saved. (*Ps. 80:3.*)

Promise These, the ransomed of the Lord, will go home along that road to Zion, singing the songs of everlasting joy. For them all sorrow and all sighing will be gone forever, only joy and gladness will be there. (*Is. 35:10.*)

■ *One evening the Holy Spirit is obviously working in a group of young Christians who some time ago accepted*

Jesus Christ as their Saviour. On this particular evening they come to full surrender, and accept Him as their Victor. 'Thanks be to God, which giveth us the victory through our Lord Jesus Christ' (1 Cor. 15:57).

One asks, 'What is expected of us now?'

'The Lord will show you. Wait patiently for His guidance. But there is one thing I can advise you to do now, and that is to organise prayer cells. Prayer is not a prefix or a suffix; it is central. Over the whole world I see that God gives His children prayer cells. It is not only the Communists who form cells, but wherever two or three come together in Jesus' name, there is a cell for Him. In eternity we shall see how important prayer meetings have been.' (Not Good If Detached.)

8

Prayer Oh, that you would wonderfully bless me and help me in my work. (*1 Chron. 4:10.*)

Promise Commit everything you do to the Lord. Trust him to help you do it and he will. (*Ps. 37:5.*)

9

Prayer Help me never to tell a lie. (*Prov. 30:8.*)

Promise When the Holy Spirit, who is truth, comes, he shall guide you into all truth. (*John 16:13.*)

10

Prayer Save your beloved people from these beasts. (*Ps. 74:19.*)

Promise The needs of the needy shall not be ignored forever; the hopes of the poor shall not always be crushed. (*Ps. 9:18.*)

11

Prayer   Pity me, O Lord, for I am weak. My eyes are growing old and dim from grief. (*Ps. 6:2, 7.*)

Promise   Although God gives him grief, yet he will show compassion too, according to the greatness of his loving-kindness. (*Lam. 3:32.*)

12

Prayer   Don't toss me aside, banished forever from your presence. (*Ps. 51:11.*)

Promise   Don't be afraid, for the Lord will go before you and will be with you; he will not fail nor forsake you. (*Deut. 31:8.*)

13

Prayer   Make everyone rejoice who puts his trust in you. (*Ps. 5:11.*)

Promise   The meek will be filled with fresh joy from the Lord, and the poor shall exult in the Holy One of Israel. (*Is. 29:19.*)

14

Prayer   Give me your instructions. Make me understand what you want. (*Ps. 119:26, 27.*)

Promise   The Lord grants wisdom! His every word is a treasure of knowledge and understanding. (*Prov. 2:6.*)

■ *Trying to catch up on our prayers while sitting in the bus or train or aeroplane after the day's work has begun is a poor substitute. We must begin the day by tuning our instruments with the help of the great Conductor. Prayer is the key for the day; the lock for the night. When Satan cannot keep us from doing work for the Lord he comes behind us and pushes us into doing too much work, and much we do is not right.*

You can do more than praying after you have prayed. You can never do more than praying before you have prayed. (Not Good If Detached.)

15

Prayer   God, be merciful to me, a sinner. (*Luke 18: 13.*)

Promise   He is merciful and tender toward those who don't deserve it; he is slow to get angry and full of kindness and love. (*Ps. 103:8.*)

16

Prayer   O God, don't stay away! Come quickly! Help! (*Ps. 72:12.*)

Promise   There is none like the God of Jerusalem — He descends from the heavens in majestic splendour to help you. (*Deut. 33:26.*)

17

Prayer   In your wrath, remember mercy. (*Hab. 3:2.*)

Promise   Though I destroyed you in my anger, I will have mercy on you through my grace. (*Is. 60:10.*)

18

Prayer My eyes are straining to see your promises come true. When will you comfort me with your help? (*Ps. 119:82.*)

Promise The Lord will again comfort Jerusalem. (*Zech. 1:17.*)

19

Prayer May I never forget your words; for they are my only hope. (*Ps. 119:43.*)

Promise The Holy Spirit ... will teach you much, as well as remind you of everything I myself have told you. (*John 14:26.*)

20

Prayer Hear the cry of your beloved child — come with mighty power and rescue me. (*Ps. 108:6.*)

Promise Everyone who calls upon the name of the Lord will be saved. (*Joel 2:32.*)

21

Prayer Help us, God of our salvation! Help us for the honour of your name. (*Ps. 79:9.*)

Promise I will deliver you. (*Jer. 39:17.*)

▆ *The cell door closed after me, and I was once more alone.*

'How did it go?'

'Was it bad?'

'Did you mention any names?'

The questions came anxiously through the small aperture

*in the wall under the table. I could set their minds at ease.
'No, it was not at all bad.'*

I told of his building a fire, and of the easy hearing.

*'It's incredible! Do watch yourself. Don't trust him.
Use all of your free time from now on to plan what you
will say at your next hearing.'*

*That recalled my first day in Cell 397, when I had been
given the same advice. My answer then had been, 'That is
unnecessary, for the Lord promises us in His Word that if
we are brought before rulers and kings He will give to us,
through His Spirit, whatsoever we shall speak.' (A
Prisoner And Yet.)*

22

Prayer   Don't bring me to trial! For as compared
with you, no one is perfect. (*Ps. 143:2.*)

Promise   Who dares accuse us whom God has chosen
for his own? Will God? No! He is the one who has
forgiven us and given us right standing with himself.
Who will then condemn us? Will Christ? No! For he
is the one who died for us. (*Rom. 8:33, 34.*)

23

Prayer   O Lord Jehovah, remember me again —
please strengthen me. (*Judges 16:28.*)

Promise   They that wait upon the Lord shall renew
their strength. (*Is. 40:31.*)

24

Prayer I will sing of your forgiveness, for my lips will be unsealed — oh, how I will praise you. (*Ps. 51: 15.*)

Promise The Lord will show the nations of the world his justice; all will praise him. (*Is. 61:11.*)

25

Prayer Now hear my prayers; oh, listen to my cry, for my life is full of troubles, and death draws near. (*Ps. 88:2, 3.*)

Promise The Lord hears the good man when he calls to him for help, and saves him out of all his troubles. (*Ps. 34:17.*)

26

Prayer O Lord, forgive your people Israel whom you have redeemed. (*Deut. 21:8.*)

Promise If my people will humble themselves and pray, and search for me, and turn from their wicked ways, I will hear them from heaven and forgive their sins and heal their land. (*2 Chron. 7:14.*)

27

Prayer Has the Lord rejected me forever? Will he never again be favourable? (*Ps. 77:7.*)

Promise The Lord will not abandon him forever. (*Lam. 3:31.*)

Prayer Lord, I trust in you alone. Don't let my enemies defeat me. (*Ps. 31:1.*)

Promise My people shall never again be dealt a blow like this. (*Joel 2:27.*)

█ *Hundreds of refugees were living in a big factory. There was a strong feeling of opposition toward all Christians. A newspaper had been posted near the entrance stating that no one who called himself a Christian would be permitted to enter the place.*

I went to the police and inquired about the possibility of having myself registered as a refugee. I was registered and walked into the factory right past the prohibitory paper.

My suitcase of cares was full to the brim, and when I emptied it before the Lord I prayed, 'Lord, here they are; help me now to leave them with Thee and continue my way unburdened.'

Suddenly out of the confusion of sounds around me a conversation struck my ear. On the other side of the paper partition two men were planning how they would deal with a Christian who might be bold enough to enter the building.

I didn't hear the end of their discussion. The last thought which came to mind was 'Underneath me are His eternal arms.' (Amazing Love.)

29

Prayer Don't let them kill me! Rescue me from their clutches. (*Jer. 15:15.*)

Promise I will come and do for you all the good things I have promised. (*Jer. 29:10.*)

30

Prayer   'But I'm not the person for a job like that!'
Moses exclaimed. (*Ex. 3:11.*)
Promise   I will tell you what to do. (*Ex. 4:15.*)

31

Prayer   O Lord, take away our sins. (*Hos. 14:2.*)
Promise   Your sins are all forgiven. (*Is. 6:7.*)

November

1

Prayer   Turn us around and bring us back to you
again! That is our only hope! Give us back the joys we
used to have! (*Lam. 5:21.*)

Promise   They shall be my people and I will be their
God, for they shall return to me with great joy. (*Jer. 24:
7.*)

2

Prayer   Why do you forget us forever? Why do you
forsake us for so long? (*Lam. 5:20.*)

Promise   For a brief moment I abandoned you. But
with great compassion I will gather you. (*Is. 54:7.*)

3

Prayer   Stand ready to help me. (*Ps. 119:173.*)

Promise   You will hear us and rescue us. (*2 Chron.
20:9.*)

4

Prayer 'O Lord,' she cries, 'see my plight. The enemy has triumphed.' (*Lam. 1:9.*)

Promise Don't be afraid. Just stand where you are and watch, and you will see the wonderful way the Lord will rescue you today. (*Ex. 14:13.*)

■ *Many people turn to the sin of sorcery and witchcraft, so whenever I have a full week of meetings, one evening is reserved for proving from the Bible the sin of this practice. How great a joy it is to bring the Good News of Jesus' victory into this darkness. But whenever I give this message I am so tired I can hardly reach my bed. My heart beats irregularly, and I feel I am not at all well.*

One evening I have a long talk with my heavenly Father. 'I cannot continue like this, dear Lord. Why must I testify against this particular sin?' Then I read, 'Be not afraid, but speak, and hold not thy peace: for I am with thee, and no man shall set on thee to hurt thee' (Acts 18: 9, 10).

I pray, 'Lord, I will obey, I will not fear and be silent.' (Not Good If Detached.)

5

Prayer Make me understand what you want; for then I shall see your miracles. (*Ps. 119:27.*)

Promise You will hear a Voice behind you say, 'No, this is the way; walk here.' (*Is. 30:21.*)

6

Prayer Grant us your salvation. (*Ps. 85:7.*)
Promise Salvation comes from God. What joys he
gives to all his people! (*Ps. 3:8.*)

7

Prayer Give us gladness in proportion to our former
misery! Replace the evil years with good. (*Ps. 90:15.*)
Promise The Lord himself, the King of Israel, will
live among you! At last your troubles will be over —
you need fear no more. (*Zeph. 3:15.*)

8

Prayer Let me see your kindness to me in the
morning. (*Ps. 143:8.*)
Promise Day by day the Lord also pours out his
steadfast love upon me. (*Ps. 42:8.*)

9

Prayer O Lord, don't stay away. O God my
Strength, hurry to my aid. (*Ps. 22:19.*)
Promise God is our refuge and strength, a tested
help in times of trouble. (*Ps. 46:1.*)

10

Prayer We have no way to protect ourselves against
this mighty army. We don't know what to do, but we
are looking at you. (*2 Chron. 20:12.*)
Promise Don't be afraid of the nations there, for the
Lord your God will fight for you. (*Deut. 3:22.*)

11

Prayer Lord, you alone can heal me, you alone can save, and my praises are for you alone. (*Jer. 17:14.*)

Promise I will heal you from your sins. (*Jer. 3:22.*)

■ *I was a guest on one of the farms on the vast prairies of Kansas. The youngest daughter there was just finishing high school, and all of us planned to attend the graduation exercises the following week.*

All of us? Something was threatening to mar the joy of that happy occasion. For months past there had been dissension between the father and his eldest son. The mother told me the whole story in confidence. We prayed together about it, and then I waited for the opportunity I knew God would prepare for me.

One afternoon I went riding. The whole family stood watching as I mounted. Then the father rode up alongside of me, and before I knew it, there it was, the opportunity for which we had prayed.

'Have you ever prayed "forgive us our debts as we forgive our debtors?"' I asked him. 'Do you know what has become of your sins? If you believe in Jesus Christ and belong to Him, they have been cast into the depths of the sea, and that's very deep. But then He expects also that you will forgive the sins of your boy and cast them into the depths of the sea. Don't you think you should forgive him right now?'

After we had been riding for some time in silence, he said suddenly, 'I'm going to see my son tonight. Will you go with me?'

*And so we did. The father put his hand on the shoulder
of the young man and said — was I hearing correctly? —
'My boy, will you forgive me?' (Amazing Love.)*

12

Prayer Take away the awful stain of my trans-
gressions. (*Ps. 51:1.*)

Promise I, yes, I alone am he who blots away your
sins for my own sake, and will never think of them
again. (*Is. 43:25.*)

13

Prayer Make your people always want to obey you,
and see to it that their love for you never changes. (*1
Chron. 29:18.*)

Promise I will inscribe my laws upon their hearts,
so that they shall want to honour me; then they shall
truly be my people and I will be their God. (*Jer. 31:33.*)

14

Prayer Come and have mercy on me as is your way
with those who love you. (*Ps. 119:132.*)

Promise I will look with pity on the man who has a
humble and a contrite heart. (*Is. 66:2.*)

15

Prayer Pour out your love and kindness on us, Lord,
and grant us your salvation. (*Ps. 85:7.*)

Promise God loved the world so much that he gave
his only Son so that anyone who believes in him shall
not perish but have eternal life. (*John 3:16.*)

16

Prayer All those who know your mercy, Lord, will count on you for help. (*Ps. 9:10.*)

Promise They shall never be disappointed in their God through all eternity. (*Is. 45:17.*)

17

Prayer I am yours! Save me! (*Ps. 119:94.*)

Promise You shall name him Jesus (meaning 'Saviour'), for he will save his people from their sins. (*Matt. 1:21.*)

18

Prayer Give us back the joys we used to have! (*Lam. 5:21.*)

Promise He will give: Beauty for ashes; joy instead of mourning; praise instead of heaviness. (*Is. 61:3.*)

■ *The Bible is a cheque book. When you said 'yes' to Jesus Christ, many promises were deposited to your credit at that very moment, and they were signed by the Lord Jesus Himself. But now you have to cash your cheques in order to profit by them. When you come upon such a promise and say, 'Thank you, Lord, I accept this,' then you have cashed a cheque, and that very day you'll be richer than you were the day before. (Amazing Love.)*

Prayer May my spoken words and unspoken thoughts be pleasing even to you, O Lord my Rock and my Redeemer. (*Ps. 19:14.*)

Promise True praise is a worthy sacrifice; this really honours me. Those who walk my paths will receive salvation from the Lord. (*Ps. 50:23.*)

20

Prayer Hear them from heaven and forgive them. (*1 Kings 8:36.*)

Promise If we confess our sins to him, he can be depended on to forgive us and to cleanse us from every wrong. (*1 John 1:9.*)

21

Prayer Lord, how long shall the wicked be allowed to triumph and exult? (*Ps. 94:3.*)

Promise Never envy the wicked! Soon they fade away like grass and disappear. (*Ps. 37:1, 2.*)

22

Prayer Arise, O God and scatter all your enemies! Chase them away! (*Ps. 68:1.*)

Promise The Lamb will conquer them; for he is Lord over all lords, and King of kings. (*Rev. 17:14.*)

23

Prayer Oh, save us, God of our salvation. (*1 Chron. 16:35.*)

Promise Israel shall be saved by Jehovah with eternal salvation. (*Is. 45:17.*)

24

Prayer Don't forsake me. (*Ps. 71:18.*)

Promise I will not abandon you or fail to help you. (*Josh. 1:5.*)

25

Prayer 'Save me,' I cry, 'for I am obeying.' (*Ps. 119: 146.*)

Promise He fulfils the desires of those who reverence and trust him; he hears their cries for help and rescues them. (*Ps. 145:19.*)

A quarrel was going on in the room. A Polish woman and a Belgian were lying together on a cot 27½ inches wide. Is it a wonder that conflicts arose?

The women were screaming at each other, fighting and trying to throw each other off the bed. Others meddled in the quarrel, and the shouting grew louder.

Betsie seized my arm. 'We must pray, Corrie; only the Lord can help us.' And then she prayed, 'Lord, remove this spirit of contention from the room. It is too strong for these poor people. They are so unhappy and so irritated. But Thou art the Conqueror. Let Thy grace touch the hearts of these women. Let Thy Spirit fill our souls.'

Like a storm that is stilled, the voices subsided; a cry or two, and all was quiet. How great is the power of prayer! (A Prisoner And Yet.)

26

Prayer Open my eyes to see wonderful things in your Word. (*Ps. 119:18.*)

Promise Out of their gloom and darkness the blind will see my plans. (*Is. 29:18.*)

27

Prayer 'O Lord,' I prayed, 'be kind and heal me, for I have confessed my sins.' (*Ps. 41:4.*)

Promise I have seen what they do, but I will heal them anyway! (*Is. 57:18.*)

28

Prayer Don't let them scorn me for obeying you. (*Ps. 119:22.*)

Promise He will vindicate you with the blazing light of justice shining down as from the noonday sun. (*Ps. 37:6.*)

29

Prayer Oh, that the time of their rescue were already here! (*Ps. 14:7.*)

Promise The ends of the earth shall see the salvation of our God. (*Is. 52:10.*)

30

Prayer Bend down and hear my prayer, O Lord, and answer me, for I am deep in trouble. (*Ps. 86:1.*)

Promise It is he who will supply all your needs from his riches in glory, because of what Christ Jesus has done for us. (*Phil. 4:19.*)

December

1

Prayer For you are the Fountain of life; our light is from your Light. Pour out your unfailing love on those who know you! (*Ps. 36:9, 10.*)

Promise Eternal life is in him and this life gives light to all mankind. (*John 1:4.*)

2

Prayer O Lord, please help us. Save us. (*Ps. 118:25.*)

Promise Though I am surrounded by troubles you will bring me safely through them. You will clench your fist against my angry enemies! (*Ps. 138:7.*)

◼ *Betsie and I decided never to talk about food. We had observed that there were many demons in our environment, and were reminded of the text: 'This kind can come forth by nothing but by prayer and fasting.' We decided to link up our involuntary fasting with our spiritual endeavours. The result was that we did not suffer because of the poor food; it even tasted good much of the time. The blessings we received upon our struggle against the evil powers around us we ascribed to our fasting. It was so wonderful that we had to do with a loving Saviour. We talked it over with Him and, though we did not clearly understand this problem ourselves, we left it in His hands and worked quietly on. (A Prisoner And Yet.)*

3

Prayer   Don't leave me to the mercy of my enemies. (*Ps. 119:121.*)

Promise   Be strong, fear not, for your God is coming to destroy your enemies. He is coming to save you. (*Is. 35:4.*)

4

Prayer   Will God really live upon the earth with men ? (*2 Chron. 6:18.*)

Promise   God has said of you, 'I will live in them and walk among them, and I will be their God and they shall be my people.' (*2 Cor. 6:16.*)

5

Prayer   Look down in love upon me. (*Ps. 119:135.*)

Promise   Nothing will ever be able to separate us from the love of God demonstrated by our Lord Jesus Christ when he died for us. (*Rom. 8:39.*)

6

Prayer   Don't leave me now, for trouble is near. (*Ps. 22:11.*)

Promise   I am with you always, even to the end of the world. (*Matt. 28:20.*)

7

Prayer Rescue me, O God, from these unjust and cruel men. (*Ps. 71:4.*)

Promise Yes, I will certainly deliver you from these wicked men and rescue you from their ruthless hands. (*Jer. 15:21.*)

8

Prayer So do as you have promised! Bless me and my family forever! (*2 Sam. 7:29.*)

Promise He will love you and bless you and make you into a great nation. (*Deut. 7:19.*)

9

Prayer Let the Lord our God favour us and give us success. (*Ps. 90:17.*)

Promise Commit your work to the Lord, then it will succeed. (*Prov. 16:3.*)

■ *One evening the conversation is about prayer. Lailani says, 'I think it is very difficult to pray.'*

'No wonder. Even the disciples did not find it easy. They asked the Lord to teach them how to pray. It is a strategic point. The devil smiles when we are up to our ears in work, but he trembles when we pray. Sometimes I think that there must be a map of the world both in heaven and in hell. The most important points on the map are not the Kremlin in Moscow or the Pentagon building in Washington, but the places where two or three or more are gathered in Jesus' name in prayer meetings.' (Not Good If Detached.)

10

Prayer Let your favour shine again upon your servant. (*Ps. 31:16.*)

Promise The good man walks along in the ever-brightening light of God's favour; the dawn gives way to morning splendour. (*Prov. 5:18.*)

11

Prayer Hear my cry, for I am very low. (*Ps. 142:6.*)

Promise The eternal God is your Refuge, and underneath are the everlasting arms. (*Deut. 33:27.*)

12

Prayer Don't abandon me — for you made me. (*Ps. 138:8.*)

Promise The Lord will work out his plans for my life. (*Ps. 138:8.*)

13

Prayer Be our strength each day and our salvation in the time of trouble. (*Is. 33:2.*)

Promise The Lord saves the godly! He is their salvation and their refuge when trouble comes. (*Ps. 37:39.*)

14

Prayer Lord Jesus, receive my spirit. (*Acts 7:59.*)

Promise There are many homes up there where my Father lives, and I am going to prepare them for your coming. When everything is ready, then I will come and get you so that you can always be with me where I am. (*John. 14:30*)

15

Prayer My soul claims the Lord as my inheritance. (*Lam. 3:24.*)

Promise I am their heritage! (*Ezek. 44:28.*)

16

Prayer Please forgive this foolish wickedness of mine. (*2 Sam. 24:10.*)

Promise See, I have taken away your sins. (*Zech. 3:4.*)

■ *The blood of Jesus Christ has great power! There is perhaps not a word in the Bible that is so full of secret truths as the blood of Jesus. It is the secret of His incarnation, when Jesus took our flesh and blood; the secret of His obedience unto death, when He gave His blood at the Cross of Calvary; the secret of His love that went beyond all understanding, when He bought us with His blood; the secret of His victory over the enemy and the secret of our eternal salvation. Why does the devil hate this world? Because it reminds him of his defeat on Calvary by the death of Jesus who gave His blood for us, but also it reminds him of Jesus' life, the resurrected one, to whom we always may come with our sins. That is why the devil is afraid of it. The blood of Jesus Christ has great power. (Marching Orders.)*

17

Prayer Decree victories for your people. (*Ps. 4:4.*)

Promise The good man does not escape all troubles — he has them too. But the Lord helps him in each and every one. (*Ps. 34:19.*)

18

Prayer Bring me out of prison, so that I can thank you. (*Ps. 142:7.*)

Promise He gives families to the lonely, and releases prisoners from jail, singing with joy! (*Ps. 68:6.*)

19

Prayer Lord, you promised to let me live! (*Ps. 119: 116.*)

Promise If they fall it isn't fatal, for the Lord holds them with his hand. (*Ps. 37:24.*)

20

Prayer Look down in pity and grant strength to your servant and save me. (*Ps. 86:16.*)

Promise Once again you will have compassion on us. (*Mic. 7:19.*)

21

Prayer I look to you for help, O Lord God. You are my refuge. Don't let them slay me. (*Ps. 141:8, 9.*)

Promise I will guard and support you. (*Is. 42:6.*)

22

Prayer Don't let me die half through my years! (*Ps. 102:24.*)

Promise I, Wisdom, will make the hours of your day more profitable and the years of your life more fruitful. (*Prov. 9:11.*)

23

Prayer   Oh, have pity and help me. (*Ps. 30:10.*)

Promise   I am holding you by your right hand — I, the Lord your God — and I say to you, Don't be afraid; I am here to help you. (*Is. 41:13.*)

■ *There was a woman tourist in Bermuda who used her vacation time not only for rest and recreation but also for spreading the Gospel. It was a time of great blessing for her and after returning to her home town, she was faithful in intercession for the people living in that beautiful island. Together with her prayer group, she prayed that many of them would accept the Gospel.*

Is there any better preparation for revival than that of a group of people praying with one accord? Can there be work more important than intercessory prayer? (Amazing Love.)

24

Prayer   Just tell me what to do, and I will do it, Lord. (*Ps. 119:34.*)

Promise   Trust the Lord completely; don't ever trust yourself. In everything you do, put God first and he will direct you and crown your efforts with success. (*Prov. 3:5, 6.*)

25

Prayer   I am depending on you, O Lord my God, to save me. (*Ps. 7:1.*)

Promise   He will send them a Saviour — and he shall deliver them. (*Is. 19:20.*)

26

Prayer O Lord, deliver me from evil men . . . Keep me out of their power. (*Ps. 140:1, 4.*)

Promise We live within the shadow of the Almighty, sheltered by the God who is above all gods. (*Ps. 91:1.*)

27

Prayer Now I can die content! (*Luke 2:29.*)

Promise God is taking them away from evil days ahead. For the godly who die shall rest in peace. (*Is. 57: 1, 2.*)

28

Prayer In mercy save me. (*Ps. 26:11.*)

Promise As for those who serve the Lord, he will redeem them. (*Ps. 34:22.*)

29

Prayer Don't leave me now. Don't forsake me, O God of my salvation. (*Ps. 27:9.*)

Promise He will give you another Comforter, and he will never leave you. (*John 14:16.*)

30

Prayer Remember your promise! For the land is full of darkness and cruel men. (*Ps. 74:20.*)

Promise As the waters fill the sea, so shall the earth be full of the knowledge of the Lord. (*Is. 11:9.*)

■ *The moment we are born into the very family of God all promises of the Bible are written in our names and signed by Jesus Christ. (Not Good If Detached.)*

31

Prayer Don't leave me, Lord; don't go away! (*Ps. 38:21.*)

Promise He will never abandon his people. They will be kept safe forever. (*Ps. 37:28.*)